Learn Swift Programming by Examples

Zhimin Zhan

Learn Swift Programming by Examples

Zhimin Zhan

ISBN 1505895898

Contents

Preface

On December 8, 2013, US President Barack Obama "asked every American to give it a shot to learn to code" (watch it here[1]), kicking off the Hour of Code campaign for Computer Science Education Week 2013. "Learning these skills isn't just important for your future, it's important for our country's future," President Obama said.

In February 2013, Mark Zuckerberg and Bill Gates and several other big names in IT "want kids to learn code" (video[2]). I particularly like the quote at the beginning of the video:

> "Everybody in this country should learn how to program a computer... because it teaches you how to think." - Steve Jobs

You don't have to be an American to get the message: coding (aka. programming) is an important skill for this information age. Besides the importance of programming, the other message those VIPs also tried to convey is that "you can do it".

Learning programming is a way to master communication with computers, by giving them instructions to perform tasks for you. A programming language is a language that is used to write instructions for computers to understand and execute. There are several popular programming languages such as Java, C#, Ruby, and PHP. For beginners, don't fixate on one. Computers internally work the same way, mastering thinking in programming is more important than an individual language. In my opinion, different programming languages are like dialects. I learned and taught myself over a dozen of programming languages. Once you have mastered one, it is easy to learn another.

In this book, I will use Swift, a new programming language from Mac OS X and iOS. Swift was first unveiled at the Apple Worldwide Developers Conference (WWDC) 2014, Apple describes Swift as "a successor to both the C and Objective-C languages"[3] on its website. Before Swift, Objective-C was the only programming language you could use to build Mac and iOS apps. Redmonk programming language rankings for 2015[4] shows a huge growth in

---

[1]https://www.adafruit.com/blog/2013/12/09/president-obama-calls-on-every-american-to-learn-code/
[2]http://www.psfk.com/2013/02/mark-zuckerberg-bill-gates-coding-school.html
[3]https://developer.apple.com/swift
[4]http://redmonk.com/sogrady/2015/01/14/language-rankings-1-15/

popularity for Apple's new Swift development language. According to the results, Swift went from the 68th most popular language last quarter (when it launched) to the 22nd, a jump of 46 spots which is "unprecedented in the history of these rankings."

In June 8, 2015 at WWDC 2015, Apple announced that the company is open-sourcing the Swift 2.0[5]. "We think Swift is the next big programming language, the one that we'll all be doing application and system programming on for 20 years to come," Craig Federighi, Apple's senior vice president of software engineering, said. "We think Swift should be everywhere and used by everyone."

What do these mean? Swift will be the main programming (replacing Objective-C) for coding applications for Apple's iOS, Mac OS and tvOS platforms, and developers like it. A good news for beginners, comparing to Objective-C, Swift is a lot easier to learn. So learn and master Swift, as President Obama said in the video, "Don't just download the latest app, help design it; Don't just play on your phone, program it".

What is unique about this book?

A typical how-to-program book will go through the programming concepts, syntax and followed by demonstrations with simple examples. I have read dozens of them (for different programming languages or tools) before and have taught this way at universities. It was not an effective approach. It is more like a teacher dumping knowledge upon students. But I did not know a better way, until I discovered The Michel Thomas Method[6].

The Michel Thomas Method was developed by Michel Thomas for teaching foreign languages. Thomas claimed that his students could "achieve in three days what is not achieved in two to three years at any college". My understanding of this method is that the teacher starts with a simple conversation scenario, then gradually expands the scenario with a few new words each time. That way, students are familiar with the conversation topic and the majority of words or sentences, while learning some new, in real interesting conversations.

I believe this teaching method can be applied to programming. Not only a programming language may also be considered as 'a language', but also very practical. The 'conversation' in speaking languages are exercises in programming. People learn better when they get satisfaction or feedbacks and see their programs works..

As I said before, thinking in programming is much more important than being familiar with a programming language. There is no better way than writing real programs for real exercises.

---

[5]https://developer.apple.com/swift/blog/?id=29
[6]http://www.michelthomas.com/

In this book, I have chosen the exercises that are very simple to understand, besides teaching values, they are useful and fun to do.

There are also some programming quiz books. I often find some of those exercises are long and hard to understand. Quite commonly, the authors seem to be fond of showing off their programming skills or smart solutions. It won't be the case in this book. This book is a guide to programming and its purpose is to teach. After you finish all the exercises, you will be able to write working (might not be perfect) programs, and with confidence to continue to learn and grow.

Who should read this book

Every one who wants to write apps (and games) for Mac OS X, iOS, watchOS and tvOS. In particular, I would strongly encourage young people to give it a go.

How to read this book

It is highly recommended to read this book from page to page. The exercises are organized into chapters, exercises within each chapter generally follows an 'easy-to-hard' pattern.

The solutions for all exercises are listed in Appendix 2, and also can be downloaded on the book website[7], refer to Resources for access.

Send me feedback

We'd appreciate your comments, suggestions, reports on errors in the book and code. You may submit your feedback on the book site.

Zhimin Zhan

Brisbane, Australia

---

[7]http://zhimin.com/books/learn-swift-programming-by-examples

1. Introduction

I still remember my first programming lesson. The first sentence the coach said was "computers are not mysterious". Nobody uses the term 'mysterious' to describe computers nowadays. It was the case in 1980's, computers were rare back then.

We are in the "Information Age" now, where computers are a large part of our lives. It seems to me that programming remains mysterious and difficult to the majority of people despite the fact that they spend most of their working hours in front of computers.

Once you have mastered programming, there are many things you can do, such as:

- Instantly rename hundreds of file with a script instead of doing it one by one
- Generate a nice Excel report from raw data instead of typing it in
- Write a document once and use scripts to generate several different formats: HTML (online), PDF, ePub and Kindle
- Turn on or off certain electronic devices when a certain condition is met
- Write a cool iOS App or game

The bottom line is that when you know how software works you will definitely use computers better.

Before we start, just like my coach, I am telling you that "programming is not mysterious" and you can master it. I believe this book can guide you to the wonderful programming world.

Like many skills, you cannot master programming by reading the book only, you need to **do it**. Let's begin.

1.1 Xcode

Coding Swift requires Xcode 6 or later installed on a Mac computer. Xcode is the integrated development environment (IDE) for developing software for OS X and iOS. Xcode[1] (the latest version to date is 8.0) is available free of charge on the Mac App Store.

---

[1]https://developer.apple.com/xcode/downloads/

Dedicated folder for coding exercises

I suggest creating a dedicated folder to put all your code (for the exercises in this book) in, for example, `/Users/YOURUSERNAME/swiftcode`.

1.2 Swift Playgrounds in Xcode

Swift Playgrounds, as its name suggests, is an interactive playground for trying out Swift. In playground, Xcode evaluates code as you write it.

Start a new Playground

1. In Xcode, select menu "File" → "New" → "Playground..."

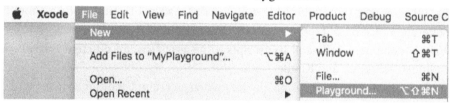

2. Select target platform and template

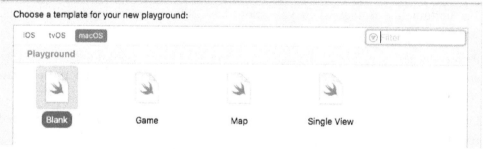

3. Choose the location to save the playground
4. Playground is shown

The code in on the left and evaluated output on the right (in a slight darker background).

You are ready to go, type in some Swift code. Xcode supports IntelliSense, i.e. providing code competition and code suggestions.

```
5 var str = "Hello, playground"
6 print( items: Any... )
Void print(items: Any...)
Void print(items: Any..., separator: String, terminator: String)
Void print(items: Any..., separator: String, terminator: String, toStream: &Target)
Void print(items: Any..., toStream: &Target)
```

Show output console

In Xcode Playground, the output of each statement will be shown on the right pane (gray one). To display the whole program's output, which is always a good idea, show the Debug area as below.

1.3 Swift Projects in Xcode

More commonly, we organize code and related files in a folder structure, known as "Project". When we a Xcode project file (with extension .xcodeproj) in Xcode, all the files in the project are included.

Create a new project

1. In Xcode, select menu "File" → "New" → "Project..."

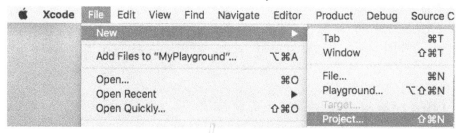

2. Select a project template.

   There are quite a number of combinations.

   - **macOS - Command Line Tool**

     The application for running from command line. This will be main project type we will be using up to Chapter 10.

   - **macOS - Cocoa App**

     GUI application on Mac computers.

   - **iOS**

     Apps running on iPhone and iPad.

3. Enter project name and select destination folder

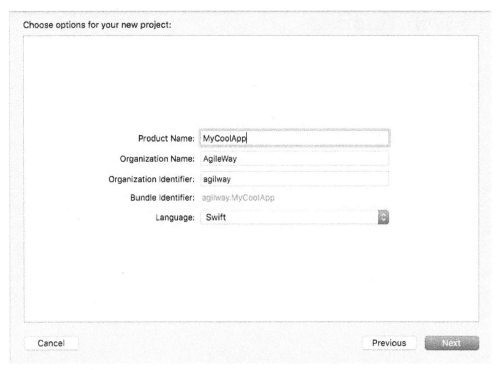

Choose options for your new project:

Product Name: MyCoolApp

Organization Name: AgileWay

Organization Identifier: agilway

Bundle Identifier: agilway.MyCoolApp

Language: Swift

Cancel   Previous   Next

4. Project created

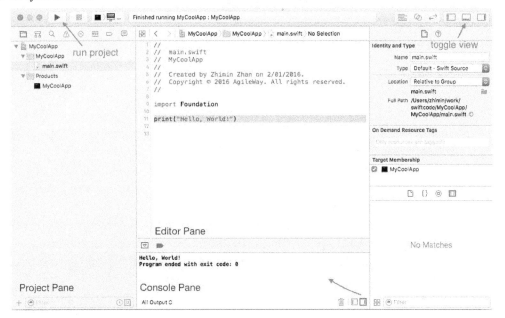

1.4 Swift Tutorials

While I believe you can learn basic Swift programming with this book, there are online tutorials that you may use as supplement. For example, read them on your iPad while waiting at bus stops. Here are two good (and free) ones.

 Why bother this book if I can get 'The Swift Programming Language' book free?

Online tutorials teach you the basic Swift syntax and some programming concepts. While they are important, these knowledge is only be useful if can be put into practice. For example, to be a good chess player, knowing chess rules is not enough.

Programming, in my opinion, is a problem solving skill to solve problems in a computer friendly way. This knowledge can only gained by actual coding, which is what this book for. Online tutorials, especially video tutorials, put learners in a passive mode. You need a book such as this one to turn passive knowledge to your own.

1.5 Rhythm for Working on the exercises

Every exercise has 6 sections:

- **The problem to solve**. It usually comes with sample output for easier understanding. Make sure you understand it well.
- **Purpose**. What you can learn from this exercise.
- **Analyze**. Analyze a problem like a programmer. This is an important step. Quite often we know how to do it but cannot describe it well. Take number sorting as an example; you can sort 5 numbers instantly on top of your head. But how about 100 numbers? This requires you to translate your understanding of sorting step by step into procedures that a computer can execute.
- **Write the code for the exercise**. No one can learn programming by reading, you have to actually do it. You may refer to the hints section to to help you get through.
- **Hints**. I list the hints (in Swift code format) that may help you to solve the problem when you get stuck.

If you are struggling to solve an exercise, feel free to check out our solutions (at Appendix II). The exercises are selected to introduce new programming skills/practices as well as previous knowledge. So don't worry if you cannot get it right the first time, you will have chances to apply in later exercises. As long as you are trying, you are learning.

- **Solution(s)**. Solutions (can be found at Appendix II) to the most of exercises are between 20 to 50 lines of code. The runnable solution scripts can be downloaded at the book site.
- **Review**. Think about what you have learnt.

1.6 Common Errors

Programmers (new or experienced) encounter code errors every day. I don't expect you to get the exercises right at the first go. We learn from mistakes.

Typos

It is normal that we make typing mistakes when writing code. Xcode checks the syntax of code before running it. If there are syntax errors in code, the error messages are usually quite helpful for identifying the error. For example, in the code below, instead 'else' at line 10, I typed `elwe`.

```
 8   if (row < 8) {
 9       star_count = row + 1
10   } elwe {
11       star_count = 15 - row
12   }
```

Xcode highlights compile time errors.

```
 8   if (row < 8) {
 9       star_count = row + 1
10   }; elwe {                    Consecutive statements on a line must be separated by ';'
11       star_count = 15 - row
```

Issue   Consecutive statements on a line must be separated by ';'

Fix-it   Insert ";"

The error message means `elwe` is undefined (don't worry if it is not meaningful to you yet, you will understand soon). It helps identify where the error is.

No matching parenthesis or brackets.

Just like Math, if there is a left bracket "(" in code, there shall be a matching right bracket ")". There are also matching keywords for certain code structures, such as if { ... }. For example, there are two errors in the code below.

```
 8   if (row < 8) {
 9      star_count = row + 1
10   } else {
11      star_count = (15 - row
12
13
```

1. at line 11: missing ')', shall be (15 - row).
2. at line 13: missing } for if at line 8.

Code logic errors

The above two kinds of errors (called syntax errors) are relatively easy to spot, as highlighted in Xcode. The difficult errors for programmers are code logic errors. That is, the code can run without syntax errors, but does not behave as it is supposed to. The ability to debug code errors (find and fix them) separates good programmers from the average. With practice, you will get better on this.

For beginners, I have two practical tips.

1. **One step at a time**. Write a small block of code, compile and run the code immediately. This may sound uninteresting, but in practice, many find it is the most useful tip to learn coding. If newly added or changed code fragment caused the error, 'Undo' (Cmd + z in Xcode) will get back your code to previous working state.
2. **If feeling confused, restart**. For beginners, if you stuck with existing code, chances are the complexity of the code is beyond your control. Try guessing around to get computers to work as instructed (by your code) is highly unlikely. In this case, it is better to restart from scratch. For most of exercises in this book, the solution is around 30 lines anyway.

Open terminal

The best way to interact with your programs is from the command line, you might have seen these scenes in some Hollywood movies: hackers typed some commands in some text windows, and something (usually big) happened. That windows that accept user text commands are called terminals.

The application to access the command line in Mac OS X is called 'Terminal'. Open in Finder: 'Applications" → 'Utilities" → 'Terminal'.

It looks like this:

```
⊗ ⊖ ⊕            ⬆ zhimin — bash — 80×24
Last login: Sat Oct 11 14:52:49 on ttys001
MacBook:~ zhimin$
```

Type 'swift --version', then press Enter key

```
Apple Swift version 4.2 (swiftlang-1000.11.37.1 clang-1000.11.45.1)
Target: x86_64-apple-darwin17.7.0
```

The Swift version might be different on your machine, this won't matter.

```
$ cd swiftcode
$ swift hello_world.swift
```

(cd *means 'change directory';* swift filename *means running this swift file.*)

You will see the output:

```
Hello World!
```

1.7 Interactive Swift

Interactive Swift is a tool that allows the execution of Swift code with immediate response, which can be very helpful for learning Swift syntaxes and debugging simple code errors. Interactive Swift is launched from a command line, run swift from a command line window then try Swift code there.

```
$ swift
Welcome to Apple Swift version 4.2 (swiftlang-1000.11.37.1 clang-1000.11.45.1)
  1> print("Hello " + "Swift")
Hello Swift
  2>
```

To exit the application, type ":exit", ":quit", or Ctrl+D.

In Appendix 1 ('Swift in Nutshell') I summarized the core Swift syntax and usage in examples which you can conveniently run in Swift Console.

1.8 Swift evolves

Swift is a new language, its features and syntax are still evolving, probably too rapidly in my opinion. Thankfully, Xcode provides good hints for upgrading your old version of Swift code.

- **4.2**, 2018-09-17 (current stable release)
- **4.0**, 2017-09-19
- **3.0**, 2016-09-13
- **2.0**, 2015-06-08
- **1.2**, 2015-04-18
- **1.0**, 2014-09-09

For example, the common `print` method, which prints out text to console, has changed three times from 1.0 to 2.0.

```
print("Hello")                          // Swift 1
print("Hello", appendNewline: false)    // Swift 1.2
print("Hello", terminator: "")          // Swift 2
```

2. Printing Shapes

Printing out asterisk characters (*) in shapes is often used as beginner's programming exercises, as they are simple, easy to understand and visually interesting.

2.1 Print out Triangle

Write a program to print out asterisks like the triangle shape below:

```
*
**
***
****
*****
******
*******
********
*********
**********
```

Purpose

- Develop ability to analyze patterns
- Variables
- Use of looping

Analyze

Row	The number of stars
1	1
2	2
3	3
...	...
n	n

Code in Xcode Playground

The first 3 exercises are simple output text pattern ones. I recommend you coding them in Xcode Playground, simple and getting quick feedback.

Hints

Print out text.

```
print("*")
print("**") // will be in a separate line
```

Generate multiple occurrences of the same character.

```
// get multiple '$'s
String(repeating: "$", count: 3)  // => "$$$"
```

Using a variable to store an integer.

Variables

You can think of a variable is a 'labeled box' in computers to store data, its data can be changed. The syntax convention[1] for Swift variables is lower Camel Case[2], for example, myBirthDate.

```
var starCount = 2
print(String(repeating: "*", count: starCount)) // => '**'

starCount = starCount + 1 // now starCount => 3
print(String(repeating: "*", count: starCount)) // => '***'
```

Print out text multiple times in a loop (fixed number of times).

---

[1]https://github.com/raywenderlich/swift-style-guide
[2]http://c2.com/cgi/wiki?LowerCamelCase

```
for index in 1...3 {
  print(index)
}
```

Output:

```
1
2
3
```

The { ... } mark the beginning and end of loop respectively. The variable `index` is the looping index, often used in the code within the loop. `print(index)` is the code fragment that executes for specified 3 times.

 ## Working out the solution on your computer

Make sure you understand the *Analyse* and *Hints* parts before you start.

2.2 Print out a half diamond

Write a program that prints out half of the diamond shape using asterisks.

```
*
**
***
****
*****
******
*******
********
*******
******
*****
****
***
**
*
```

Purpose

- Decrement count in loops

Analyze

The key to this problem is to determine the number of stars for the corresponding rows.

```
row 1 to  8: the same as row number
row 9 to 16: 16 - row
```

Hints

Control flows using if ... else

Code, in its simplest form, is executed from top to bottom. But if there are if conditions and loops (and later methods and classes), it will change the flow of execution. The conditional expressions (if-then-else statements) run different code statements depending on a boolean condition (true or false).

```
var score = 75
if score < 60 {
  print("Failed!")
} else {
  print("Pass!")
}
```

Output:

```
Pass!
```

If you change the var score = 59 and run again, you will get Failed!.

Boolean condition

The statement score < 60 after if is called a boolean condition. Its value can only be either true or false (which are called boolean values).

Common comparison operators in Swift

==	equal to
!=	not equal to
<	less than
<=	less than or equal to
>	greater than
>=	greater than or equal to

Examples:

```
2 > 1   // => true
2 == 1  // => false  (equal to)
2 != 1  // => true   (not equal to)
2 <= 2  // => true
```

Equal sign = and Double equal sign ==

The equal sign (=) is the "assignment operator", it assigns a value to a variable on the left.

```
var a = 1 + 2  // assign 3 to a
```

Please note the "assignment operator" is different from the "equality symbol" in Math. For example, the statement below increases the value of a by 1 (*assign a new value to* a) in programming code. The same equation in Math is invalid.

```
a = a + 1  // increment a by 1
```

The double equal signs (==) is a comparison operator, it compares two values for equality (returns true if a is equal to b, false otherwise).

```
if a == b {
  print("Found a match!")
}
```

Incorrect use of = for == is one of the most common mistakes in programming[3].

---

[3]http://www.cprogramming.com/tutorial/common.html

2.3 Print out diamond shape

Print 7 rows of '*' in a diamond shape as below:

```
   *
  ***
 *****
*******
 *****
  ***
   *
```

Purpose

- Analyse more complex patterns
- Math operators

Analyze

Below are formulas to calculate the number of star; where rowNumber represents the row number and totalRows represents the total number of rows,

1. The number of stars for the rows before the middle one is (rowNumber - 1) * 2 + 1.
2. the number of stars for the rows after the middle one is (totalRows - rowNumber) * 2 + 1

Think about the spaces in front of each row, except for the 4th row (the longest middle one).

Hints

Write down the number of spaces and stars for each row.

```
row 1: print 3 spaces + 1 star
row 2: print 2 spaces + 3 stars
row 3: print 1 space  + 5 stars
row 4: print 0 space  + 7 stars
row 5: print 1 space  + 5 stars
row 6: print 2 spaces + 3 stars
row 7: print 3 spaces + 1 star
```

Math operators: multiply and divide

The Math multiply and divide operator are * and / respectively.

```
8 / 2  // => 4
9 / 2  // => 4,  ignore the remainder
(1 + 2) * 3 + 3 / 2  // => 10
```

 If you have difficulty, do it step by step. You may try to print out the top triangle first.

2.4 Print big diamond, name your size

Ask the user for the size of diamond (based on the total number of rows) and then print out a diamond shape using asterisks '*'.

```
Enter the maximum number of rows (odd number): 9
        *
       ***
      *****
     *******
    *********
     *******
      *****
       ***
        *
```

Purpose

- Read user's input into a variable
- Convert string to integer
- Use variable control loop times
- Swift optionals

Code in Xcode Project

From this exercise onwards, please code them in a Xcode project. The reason: this exercise requires user's input and this does not work in Playground.

Moreover, using Xcode project is the standard way to developer Swift App. The project type is Mac OS X : Command Line Tool For instructions of creating a Xcode project, please refer to Chapter 1.

For exercises before Chapter 11, select project template: OS X → Application → Command Line Tool.

Analyze

The size of the diamond is not fixed, it depends on the number the user entered. The number the program asks the user to enter is the total number of rows, which can be stored in an variable.

If you divide the diamond into two parts (top and bottom), work out the number of rows for each part.

Hints

Read user's input

We can use `readLine()` function to read user's input from a command line application.

```
let userInput = readLine()
```

String and Integer

The `String` and `Integer` are two most common data types.

```
var a = "12"
var b = "3"
a + b        // => "123"

var c = 12
var d = 3
c + d        // =>  15
```

Math operations, such as Add, between `String` and `Integer` will get compile error.

```
var b = "3"
var c = 12
b + c  // Binary operator '+' cannot be applied to 'String' and 'Int'
```

Convert a number string to integer

```
var a = "12"
Int(a) // => to integer 12
```

**

Swift Optionals

Optionals in Swift is quite difficult concept for me, as it is not in other languages I have used. The purpose of Optionals is to avoid assign `nil` (means no value) to a variable. It is better explained with example.

```
var str1:String
str1 = nil  // error: Nil cannot be assigned to type "string"
```

Assign `nil` to an Optional is OK, with an extra `?`.

```
var str2:String?
str2 = nil  // OK
```

However, you can force assigning an optional variable to non-optional one by using `!`.

```
var str3:String
str3 = str2 // error: Value of optional type "String?" not unwrapped
str3 = str2! // OK
```

You might still find it confusing. Good news is that Xcode will give you hints and even offer 'Fix it'.

```
 39  str3 = str2!      ⊙ Value of optional type 'String?' not unwrapped; did you mean to use '!' or '?'?
 40
 ⊙ Value of optional type 'String?' not unwrapped; did you mean to use '!' or '?'?
 Fix-It  Insert "!"
```

You must know it first, then instruct computers

Trying to enter a big number for the last program, say 99. It will print a big diamond, Wow!

This an important aspect of programming. Once you figure out the pattern and logic of a problem and translate it into computer understandable language (program), it can solve the similar problems at any scale. For example, the effort taken for computers to calculate 2 x 2 is not much different from 12343 x 35345. In other words, we (human) must understand **how** to solve the problem first. Programming translates the **how** into instructions that computers can follow.

2.5 Exercises

Write code to print out the shapes below, the width of shape is changeable.

Rhombus

```
    * * * * *
   * * * * *
  * * * * *
 * * * * *
* * * * *
```

Hollow Square

```
* * * * *
*       *
*       *
*       *
* * * * *
```

Heart

```
   * * * * *      * * * * *
  * * * * * *    * * * * * * *
 * * * * * * * *  * * * * * * * *
* * * * * * * * * * * * * * * * * * *
 * * * * * * * * * * * * * * * * *
  * * * * * * * * * * * * * * *
   * * * * * * * * * * * * *
    * * * * * * * * * * *
     * * * * * * * * *
      * * * * * * *
       * * * * *
        * * *
         *
```

Hints

The first three rows are static regardless of the size.

3. Quiz Time

We will do some computer interaction exercises.

3.1 Simple Add Calculator

Write a simple calculator that adds two integers (up to 99) from user inputs and prints out the sum.

```
I am an adding machine, and I am good at it.
Enter first number: (type 1, press Enter)
Enter second number: (type 99, press Enter)
Thinking ...
Got it, the answer is: 100
```

Purpose

- Read user's keyboard input
- Use variables for mathematic operations
- Print variable in a string

Analyze

An adding operation requires two inputs that we need to collect from the user. The user-entered number must be stored (in variables) before we can add them up and output the sum.

Hints

Read a number from user's keyboard input

```
var num1 = Int(readLine()!)
```

Print variables in string

```
var name = "Courtney"
var age  = 13
print("Hello, My name is \(name), I am \(age) years old.")
```

Output:

```
Hello, My name is Courtney, I am 13 years old.
```

3.2 Addition Quiz

 Write a program to prompt 10 single digit addition questions, provide feedback based on user's response and then print out the score.

```
1 + 1 =  (enter 2)
Correct.
2 + 7 = (enter 8)
Wrong!
...
6 + 3 =

Your score: 8/10
```

Purpose

- Generating a random number
- Looping
- Incrementing a variable (counting)

Analyze

10 questions means repeating the following operations 10 times

1. generate one number
2. generate another number
3. ask user for the answer
4. check the answer and print out feedback

To get a score, you will need to prepare a counter. If the user's input is correct, increment the counter by 1.

Hints

Random number

A random number is a computer generated number in a nondeterministic manner. Random numbers are quite useful for a variety of purposes, such as simulation in games, encryption, quiz (like this exercise), etc. To generate a random number within a range:

```
import Foundation
var num = Int.random(in: 0..<10)   // a random number between 0 to 9
```

The generated random number will be different for each run.

i> Before Swift 4.2, use `Int(arc4random_uniform(10))` to generate a random single digit number.

Counting

Incrementing the variable by 1.

```
var count = 0   // clear it first
for var i = 0; i < 5; i++ {
   count = count + 1
}
print(count) // => 5
```

Press `Ctrl+C` to terminate the program execution.

3.3 Subtraction Quiz

 Write a program to prompt 10 single digit subtraction questions, provide feedback based on user's response and then print out the score.

```
9 - 1 =  (enter 8)
Correct.
7 - 2 = (enter 8)
Wrong!
...
Your score: 8/10
```

Purpose

- Use logic control (if)
- Be consistent with changes: changing a part code here might affect there.

Analyze

It might seem like the previous exercise, however, this one can be a little tricky.

Hints

Subtraction in this context is using a bigger number to minus a smaller number. The random number generator does not guarantee the first number is bigger.

3.4 Number Guessing Game

 The computer has a secret number (0 to 9), the program prompts the user to enter a guess and give feedback such as 'too big' or 'too small'. The program ends when a correct answer is entered.

```
I have a secret number (0 - 9), Can you guess it?
=> (you type 9)
Too big!
=> (you type 4)
Too Small!
=> (you type 5)
Correct! You guessed 3 times.
```

Purpose

- Infinity looping
- Exit program or looping

Analyze

Different from the previous exercises, the number of times the computer 'prompts' is nondeterministic. The program ends when the player answered correctly.

Hints

Infinity loop

An infinity loop is a sequence of code loops endlessly.

```
while true {
  // ...
}
```

The Apple Campus is the corporate headquarters of Apple Inc., located at 1 Infinite Loop in Cupertino, California, United States.

(source Wikipedia[1])

Exit from a loop

Obviously we need an exit mechanism to make infinity loop useful.

```
while true {
  // ...
  if result > 60 {
    print("You passed")
    break
  }
}
print("made here")
```

---

[1]http://en.wikipedia.org/wiki/Infinite_Loop_%28street%29

3.5 Exercises

Hangman

Write a program to guess a word by trying to guess the individual characters. The word to be guessed shall be provided using the command-line argument.

Your program shall look like:

```
My secret word: _____

Key in one character or the guess word: a
Try 1: _____a__
Key in one character or the guess word: t
Try 2: ___t_a__
Key in one character or guess word: o
Try 3: _oot_a__
Key in one character or the guess word: football
Try 4: Correct!
You got it in 4 tries.
```

Hints

If you are not familiar with Array, come back to do this exercise after the next chapter.

4. Array and Dictionary

In previous exercises, we used simple data types Strings and Integers. There are composite data types that are collection of other types. The most common composite data types are Array and Hash. An Array is like a list and a Dictionary is like a lookup.

In this chapter, we will write some programs using Array and Dictionary. The Swift official documentation has good explanation on them and all their methods are listed, even with easy to understand examples.

- Swift Collection Types[1]

4.1 Sort Children Names

Names $\begin{smallmatrix} A \\ \vdots \\ z \end{smallmatrix}$ Ask a list of names and then output them in alphabetical order. The program ends when the user enters "0".

```
Enter child names in class: (0 to finish):
Dominic
Courtney
Anna
Angela
Ella
Toby
Emma
0

Kids in order:
Angela, Anna, Courtney, Dominic, Ella, Emma, Toby
```

[1]https://developer.apple.com/library/ios/documentation/swift/conceptual/Swift_Programming_Language/CollectionTypes.html

Purpose

- Adding data into an array
- Array sorting
- End a loop on a condition
- Display array

Analyze

There are two steps: collecting names and sorting them.

Hints

Add an element to an array

```
var usStates: [String] = []  // initialize an empty  array
var auStates: [String] = ["NSW", "VIC"]   // initialize an array with data
auStates.append("QLD")  // au_states now ["NSW", "VIC", "QLD"]
```

Sorting an array

```
var array = ["Google", "Samsung", "Apple", "Sony"]

// will sort array in ascending order
array.sort{ $0 < $1 } // => ["Apple", "Google", "Samsung", "Sony"]

// will sort array in descending order
array.sort{ $1 < $0 } // => ["Sony", "Samsung", "Google", "Apple"]
```

4.2 Get the character from given alphabetical position

A–1

Asks the user to enter a number between 1 to 26, and then print the character at the alphabetical position. The program ends when the user enters "0".

```
I know the alphabet very well, enter the alphabetical order number (integer) and
I will tell you the corresponding letter, 0 to quit:
1 (user enter)
is 'A'
5 (user enter)
is 'E'
0
Bye!
```

Purpose

- Access array element by index
- Infinite loop with exit condition

Analyze

The number of times the user can input is undetermined. So it will be an infinite loop with an exit condition: when '0' is entered.

We can use the alphabet position to look up in a predefined array for the corresponding character.

Hints

Like many programming languages, array indexing starts with 0, not 1.

```
var array = ["Google", "Apple", "Sony", "Samsung"]
array[0]  // => "Google"
array[2]  // => "Sony"
array[array.count - 1] // last one => "Samsung"
```

4.3 Calculate Average

 Ask the user to enter a set of student scores (non-negative) integers and then calculate the average. The program ends when the user enters "-1".

```
Enter scores: (enter -1 to finish):
87
94
100
56
74
67
75
88
-1

Average score : 80
```

Analyze

Calculation of the average is easy (see the hints below) by using existing Swift's array functions.

Purpose

- Add data element into an array
- Sum an array

Hints

Try to do sum first, then average. There are two ways to sum all elements in array:

```
// adding all elements in an array: classic way
var array = [1, 2, 3]
var theSum = 0
for num in array {
  theSum += num
}
print(theSum)    // => 6
```

The standard and more concise way to sum an array of numbers.

```
var theSum = array.reduce(0, combine: +)
```

4.4 What makes 100% in life?

X = Life 100%?

If we represent the alphabet numerically by identifying sequence of letters (A,B,C,...,X,Y,Z) with the percentages (1%,2%,3%,...,24%,25%,26%). A sum of each characters' value in a word is the meaning to life percentage. Then

H-A-R-D-W-O-R-K = (8+1+18+4+23+15+18+11)% = 98%

Ask user to enter an English word (or string) and calculate its meaning to life percentage.

```
Enter your word (in capital): HARDWORK
The value of meaning to life: 98%
```

 Try the words: "KNOWLEDGE", "ATTITUDE", "VIDEOGAME"

Purpose

- Use of Dictionary for looking up
- Treat string as an array

Analyze

Three main steps

1. Break up a string into a list of characters
2. For each character, find out its percentage value (integer).
3. Add all the percentage values up

Hints

Looping each character in a string

A string, in fact, is an array of characters.

```
var str = "Swift"
for character in str {
  print(character)
}
```

Output:

```
S
w
i
f
t
```

Looping array with index

```
var str = "Swift"
for (index, value) in str.enumerated() {
  // index starts 0
}
```

Get the value from a dictionary by a given key

```
var cityAbbrevs = ["LA": "Los Angeles", "NY": "New York" ]
cityAbbrevs["NY"] // => "New York"
```

4.5 Exercises

Find the Median

The Median is the "middle" of a sorted list of numbers. For example, the median of the data set 1, 1, 2, **5**, 6, 6, 9 is 5. If there is an even number of data values the median is the mean of the two data values in the middle. For example, the median of the data set 4, 2, 1, 3, 5, 4 is 3. It is the mean of *3* and *4* or, (3 + 4) /2 = 3.5.

Write a program to find the median of a list of numbers. The output shall be like this:

```
Enter a list of numbers (separated by space): 4 2 1 3 5 4
The Median is:   3.5
```

Hints

Split a string of list numbers to an integer array

```
var str = "12 15 7 8 25"
var strArray = str.componentsSeparatedByString(" ")
var numArray:[Int] = []
for numStr in strArray {
    numArray.append(Int(numStr)!)
}
```

5. Useful Utility Programs

In the chapters, we will write some utility program that might be useful to you.

5.1 Fahrenheit to Celsius Converter

Julie, an Australian, is going to USA, where different Fahrenheit temperature scales are used. Here is the Fahrenheit to Celsius formula: $T_c = \dfrac{5}{9}(T_f - 32)$.

Can you write a program for Julie to convert Fahrenheit to Celsius? The result is rounded to 2 digits after the decimal point.

```
Enter temperature in Fahrenheit: 100.5
In Celsius: 38.06
```

Purpose

- Apply math formula into programming
- Float number
- Rounding

Analyze

This is just simple calculation based on a given formula. So far our calculations are using integers only. This one has floating numbers, which are decimal numbers.

Hints

Convert a string to a float number

```
import Cocoa
("34.23" as NSString).floatValue
```

In Swift, the result of division between two integers is also the integer.

```
100 / 3  // => 33 (Int)
```

To get more precise result,

```
100.0 / 3  // => 33.3333333 (Double)
```

```
// when variables used
var a = 100
Float(a) / 3
```

Rounding

```
import Cocoa
round(37.455) // => 37 (Int)
round(37.455 * 100) / 100.0  // => 37.46
```

5.2 Personal Income Tax Calculator

 Here are Australian personal income tax rates for 2013-14.

Taxable income	Tax on this income
0 – $18,200	Nil
$18,201 – $37,000	19c for each $1 over $18,200
$37,001 – $80,000	$3,572 plus 32.5c for each $1 over $37,000
$80,001 – $180,000	$17,547 plus 37c for each $1 over $80,000
$180,001 and over	$54,547 plus 45c for each $1 over $180,000

Write a program to calculate how much tax a person needs to pay based on his or her annual salary.

```
Enter your annual income: 85000
Your personal income tax amount: $19397.0
```

Analyze

The calculation is easy. The key here is to compare the user entered amount against the thresholds (note, I used plurals here).

Purpose

- Branching using if, else if and else
- Logical operators: && and ||
- Switch statement

 Complete this exercise using if, else if and else first, then change to switch statement. Review the difference.

Hints

IF-ELSE IF

The branching concept is simple and self-explanatory.

```
var a  = 10
if a < 10 {
  print("single digit")
} else if a >= 100 {
  print("too big, I don't know")
} else  {
  print("two digits")
}
```

Output:

```
two digits
```

Logical operators

- NOT (`!a`)
- AND (`a && b`)
- OR (`a || b`)

Example:

```
var a = 10
if a != 0 && a < 10  {
  print("\(a) is a positive single digit number")
}
```

Switch statement

When dealing with a large number of possible conditions, `switch` statement is better than `if-else` in terms of code clarity.

```
var score = 70
var result = ""

switch score {
case 0...60 :
  result = "Fail"
case 60...70 :
  result = "Pass"
case 71...95 :
  result = "Pass with Distinction"
case 96, 97, 98, 99:
  result = "Distinction"
case 100:
  result = "High Distinction"
default:  // not matching any above conditions
  result = "Invalid Score"
}
print(result)  // => "Pass"
```

5.3 Word count

Emily wrote a book review, but she is not sure whether it meets the required word count. Assuming Emily's article is saved in a string, can you write a program to count the number of words?

(assuming the text is "'Practical Web Test Automation' book is great. The end.")

```
The text has 9 words.
```

Purpose

- Tokenization, split strings by separators into an array
- Count array size

Analyze

Words are separated by spaces (we will use this rule for the exercise). Counting how many spaces is not a good idea, as two consecutive spaces shall be counted as one in this case.

One way is to tokenization[1], splitting the text into tokens by whitespace characters.

Hints

Use `components` method to split a string into an array with given separator.

```
var pixarMovies = "Toy Story,A Bug's Life,Incredibles,Toy Story 2,Finding Nemo,Cars"
var pixarMovieList = pixarMovies.components(separatedBy: ",")
pixarMovieList.count // => 6
```

To split words by spaces, tabs or new lines (called white space characters).

```
var text = "Mac OS X"
var words = text.components(separatedBy: CharacterSet.whitespaces)
// => ["Mac", "OS", "X"]
```

---

[1]http://en.wikipedia.org/wiki/Tokenization

5.4 Generate Lotto Numbers

 Write a program to generate 6 Lotto numbers. Lotto numbers are between 1 and 49.

```
Your winning lotto numbers are [23, 34, 12, 6, 7, 49], good luck!
```

Purpose

- Check array whether contains an element
- Use of random number generator

Analyze

Obviously, we need randomness for the lotto numbers generated, and they have to be unique. We can use `arc4random_uniform` (see Ex3-2). However, the random number generator may generate duplicate ones.

Here is one way. Let's say, you are the picker for the lotto and have a number of buckets. Each bucket contains 49 individually numbered balls (from 1 to 49).

1. You go to the first bucket, close your eyes, pick up one ball and put on the table.
2. Go to the next bucket, close eyes, pick up another ball.
3. If this number was already on the table, put the ball back to the bucket.
4. Repeat the step 2 again until find the number is not already on the table.
5. Repeat 4 more times, then you get all 6 unique lotto numbers.

Hints

Check whether an array contains one element, i.e.. check the uniqueness.

```
var array = ["Apple", "Sony"]
array.contains("Apple") // => true
```

5.5 Number sorting

Numbers.   Ask the user to input 10 numbers, then sort them in order.

```
Please enter 10 numbers:
10
8
7
3
4
5
9
1
2
6

The numbers in order: 1, 2, 3, 4, 5, 6, 7, 8, 9, 10
```

Note: built-in sorting functions are not allowed.

Analyze

Imagine you have 5 coins with different values: 10c , 20c, 50c, $1, and $2. How do you sort the coins (from small to big)? I know it is obvious to human. But by now, you probably know that we need to translate our solution into steps that computers can understand.

Let's get back to our coin sorting problem. You pick up the first coin (from left to right) in your left hand, then compare it to the rest one by one (by picking it up in your right hand). If the one in your left hand is smaller, put the the coin in your right hand back. If the one in left hand is bigger, swap them. So that after each comparison, the one in your left hand is smaller. After one iteration, the one in your left hand is the smallest. Put this one aside. Then starting another iteration, picking up the first coin on the left until only one coin left.

Here is the pseudocode for the above:

```
for each element in the list
  current_one
  for the next one (index) to the last one (index) do
    if any one in remaining is bigger than current_one
      swap them
    end if
  end for (inside)
end for (outside)
```

Purpose

- Iterating an array
- Swapping variables
- Access elements in an array using index
- Looping an array from specific index range

Hint

Swapping variables

To swap two variables, it is traditionally (in most programming languages) done via a third variable:

```
// a and b are defined preceding code
var c = a
a = b
b = c
```

This is a common pattern and to help me remember, I used the phrase"ca-ab-bc".

Iterating an array, get the array element by index

```
for idx in 0...array.count-1 {
  // array[idx] to access the current element
}
array[0] // first one
array[array.count - 1] // last one
```

To loop an array from a specific index range

```
var array = ["A", "B", "C", "D", "E", "F", "G"]
var startingIndex = 2
for idx in startingIndex...(array.count-3)  {
  print( array[idx])
}
// will print out "C", "D", "E" (the index from 2 to 4)
```

5.6 Exercises

Convert Decimal to Hex

Write a program to convert an input decimal string into its equivalent hexadecimal. Your output shall look like:

```
Decimal number: 398
The equivalent hexadecimal number: 18E
```

Hints

Decimal to Hex

```
428 / 16  // => 26,  remain: 12
 26 / 16  // =>  1,  remain: 10
  1 / 16  // =>  0,  remain:  1
```

Convert the remains of the above based on all hex numbers ['0', '1', '2', '3', '4', '5', '6', '7,' '8', '9', 'A', 'B', 'C', 'D', 'E', 'F'], in reversing order.

```
 1  =>  1
10  =>  A
12  =>  C
```

The hexadecimal for decimal number '428' is '1AC'.

Convert Hex to Decimal

Write a program to convert an input hexadecimal string into its equivalent decimal number. Your output shall look like:

```
Hexadecimal : 1a
The equivalent decimal number for hexadecimal "1a" is 26
```

Hints

Power operator (Math)

```
pow(Double(2), Double(3)) // => 8
```

Hex to Decimal

```
// A5BE is a hex number
A5BE = 10 * (16 ** 3) + 5 * (16 ** 2) + 11 * (16 ** 1) + 14 * (16 ** 0)
     = 42430
```

Word to Phone Number Converter

On phone keypad, the alphabets are mapped to digits as follows:

	ABC(2)	DEF(3)
GHI(4)	JKL(5)	MNO(6)
PQRS(7)	TUV(8)	WXYZ(9)

Write a program thats prompts user for a String (case insensitive), and converts to a sequence of Keypad digits.

```
Enter your PhoneWords: 1800 TESTWISE
The actual phone number: 1800 83789473
```

6. Fun Math

Computers were created originally to do mathematic computation, hence it is named 'computer'. Math is an essential part of software design. I know for many, 'fun' is normally not the word to describe math. Programming, in my opinion, can add a 'fun' factor to math.

There are two-way benefits: programming allows you to understand math better and you can utilize your math skills to solve problems.

6.1 Finding Divisors

 Write a program to list all divisors of a given number (user entered).

```
Enter a number: (108)
The divisors of 108: 1, 2, 3, 4, 6, 9, 12, 18, 27, 36, 54, 108
```

Analyze

To determine whether a number is divisible by another, check the remainder of the division. 0 means divisible.

Purpose

- Determine a number is fully dividable.

Hints

Swift's modulo operator: % return the remainder of a division.

```
8 % 3    // => 2
9 % 3    // => 0
```

6.2 Finding the Highest Common Factor

Write a program to ask the user to enter two non-negative integers and then find the highest common factor (HCF).

```
Enter the first number: (8)
Enter the second number: (12)
The HCF of 8 and 12 is: 4
```

 Highest Common Factor

The largest common factor of two or more numbers is called the highest common factor. The HCF is also known as greatest common devisor (gcd). For example,

```
8 =  1 x 8 = 2 x 4
12 = 1 x 12 = 2 x 6 = 3 x 4
```

So the common factors of 8 and 12 are: 1, 2 and 4 (1, 2, 4 and 8 for 8; 1, 2, 3, 4, 6 and 12 for 12). 4 is the highest common factor.

Purpose

- Iterate an array
- Check whether an element is in an array?
- Use break or flag to indicate the mission completed in an iteration

Analyze

There are several methods to compute the HCF. I am going to focus on a simple way. As a matter of fact, this method has the most steps but it is the easiest one to understand.

1. Compute all divisors of the first number and note them down, e.g. 8 => [1, 2, 4, 8]
2. Compute all divisors of the second number and note them down, e.g, 12 => [1, 2, 3, 4, 6, 12]

3. Find the largest one in both divisors list: Starting with the list that has the largest divisor, work you way down, and check whether the divisor is also in the second. The first divisor found HCF.

 ## Knowing the answer to working out the algorithm

For the above example, Step 3 is quite obvious to human. If I ask you why, many might not be able to answer. Some might say: "It is obvious when seeing two divisor list". However, if the two numbers are 103096 and 234986, it is a different story, isn't it?

Computers are not 'afraid of' big numbers like us, they just need an algorithm in a set of steps to execute. If you know the answer, it means you know the algorithm, but may not be good at expressing it out. This takes time and practice. In my view, mastering this makes you a programmer. The best way is to start with simple examples. Imagine yourself as a computer, then work out steps on a paper.

Hints

Store divisors of each number into two separate arrays.

Sort one array from big to small order.

```
var divisors1 = [1, 2, 4, 8]
var divisors2 = divisors1.sort{ $0 > $1 } // => [8,4,2,1]
```

Iterate (i.e, go through one by one) one array (divisors1). For each element in this array (divisors1), check whether the other array (divisors2) contains it (included in divisors2). The first divisor found in both arrays is HCF.

```
var array = [1, 2, 3, 6]
array.contains(2) // => true
```

6.3 Finding the Least Common Multiple (LCM)

12 18
\/
36

Least (also sometimes called Lowest) common multiple is the smallest (non-zero) number that is a multiple of two or more examples. For example, 12 is the LCM of 6 and 4, as 12 = 6 x 2 and 12 = 3 x 4. 24 is a common multiple of 4 and 6, but is not the lowest.

```
Enter the first number: (6)
Enter the second number: (4)
The LCM for 6 and 12 is: 12
Calculation time: 0.0001 seconds
```

Now, try bigger numbers such as 4254 and 82835.

```
The LCM for 4254 and 82835 is: 352380090
Calculation time: 25.564194 seconds
```

Let's see how you can improve the calculation speed.

Purpose

- Time code execution
- Optimize program performance
- Use step for looping

Hints

A simple way is to search the number from the larger one of the two to the multiple of the two. For example,

```
for num in 6...6*4 {
  // check whether num is LCM?
}
```

The above brute-force way is not optimal. Obviously, it will take longer due to too many looping (a * b) when the two numbers are big.

One of the most effective way to speed up your program is to reduce the number of loops. For this example, it is not necessary to check each number from 6, 7 , 8, 9, 10, 11, 12, ..., 24. We just need to check every multiple of 6, i.e, 6, 12, 18, 24. Here is how to do it in Swift:

```
for var n = 6; n <= 24; n+=6 {
  print(n)
}
// will print out 6, 12, 18, 24
```

Time the code execution time

```
var startTime: NSDate = NSDate();
// code ...
var finishTime: NSDate = NSDate();
var duration = finishTime.timeIntervalSinceDate(startTime)
print("The time took is \(duration) seconds")
```

6.4 Finding Prime Numbers

Find prime numbers between 1 and 20.

```
Prime numbers (up to 20) are : 2, 3, 5, 7, 11, 13, 17, 19
```

 Prime Number

A prime number is a number that is bigger than one and has no divisors other than 1 and itself. For example, 5 is prime, since no number except 1 and 5 divides it. On the other hand, 6 is not a prime (it is a composite), since 6 = 2 x 3.

Analyze

Pseudocode is a high level description of a computer program. The idea of pseudocode is to convey how the problem shall be solved without being locked with a particular programming language. The below is a pseudocode to find prime numbers.

Pseudocode

```
for each number x in 2 .. 10
  for x with 2,3,4,5,6,..., x-1 (another loop)
    clear the flag (assuming it is prime number initially)
    if number can be divided by x (remainder is 0)
      oops, it is not a prime number
      mark a flag
      break
    end
  end inner for loop
  if no flag set
    this is a good prime number (it passed our checks)
    print out this prime number
  end
end outer for loop
```

Make sure you completely understand the logic to determine a prime number before coding.

Purpose

- Ranges to array
- Use a flag variable to store a status

Hints

Swift Range is a set of values within a specified begin and end. For example, (1...4) contains 1, 2, 3 and 4.

```
for x in 2...5 {
  print(x)
}
// will print 2, 3, 4, 5 in four lines.

// convert a range to an array
Array[2...5]  // => [2, 3, 4, 5]
```

Set a flag within a loop, and check it later. This is a common and very useful programming practice.

```
var isComposite = false
for num in 2...7 {
  if 8 % num == 0 {
    isComposite = true
    break
  }
}

if isComposite {
  print("8 is a composite number")
}
```

In above code, the variable isComposite is a flag. It was initially set to 'false' and its value may be changed by the following computation code. So later we can use its value to determine the prime numbers.

6.5 Fibonacci sequence

 Start with a pair of rabbits (one male and one female) born on January 1. Assume that all months are of equal length and that :

1. the first pair of rabbits reproduced two months after their own birth;
2. after reaching the age of two months, each pair produces a mixed pair, (one male, one female), and then another mixed pair each month thereafter; and
3. no rabbit dies.

How many pairs will there be in the end of each month of first year?

```
The number of rabbit pairs are:
1, 1, 2, 3, 5, 8, 13, 21, 34, 55, 89, 144
```

Analyze

Clearly, there is a pattern on the number of rabbit pairs. To find out a pattern, we need to work out the numbers in first several months, like below.

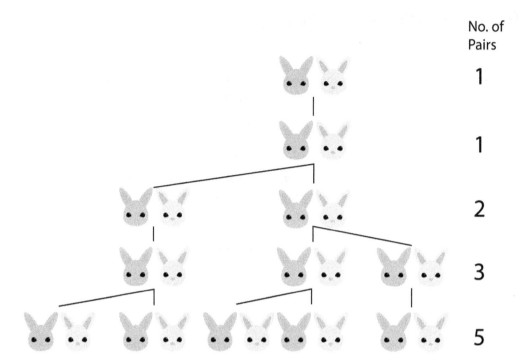

No. of
Pairs

1

1

2

3

5

 Fibonacci sequence

This is the famous 'Fibonacci sequence'. If you read the book 'Da Vinci Code', you might remember fibonacci sequence was used as the password for a safe.

Each new number in Fibonacci sequence is generated by adding the previous two numbers. By starting with 1 and 1, the first 10 numbers will be:
1, 1, 2, 3, 5, 8, 12, 21, 34, 55

Purpose

- Analyse the problem and find out its match pattern.
- Variable assignment

Hints

Fibonacci sequence starts with first 2 numbers.

```
var num1 = 1
var num2 = 1
```

The algorithm behind this program might seem simple: just produce *a number that is the sum of the previous two*. This will test your understanding of variable assignments. In programming, x = 1 is not 'x equals to 1', instead means 'assign 1 to x'. That's why we can do number increment using a = a + 1, which does not make sense in math.

```
var a = 10
a = a + 1   // now a = 11
```

The program seems simple with only a few lines of code, however, it is not as simple as you might think. If you get stuck, think about *assigning variables to a new number*.

Also, after generating a correct Fibonacci sequence, you will need to think about stopping at the 12th number (12 months).

6.6 Consecutive Sums

Some natural numbers can be written as a sum of consecutive natural numbers. For example, 10 = 1 + 2 + 3 + 4. Some can be written in more than one way. For example, 9 = 2 + 3 + 4 and 9 = 4 + 5. Now can you write a program to output all possible ways for a given natural number.

```
Enter a number: 9
9 = 2 + 3 + 4
9 = 4 + 5
```

Analyze

A plus operation involves at least 2 numbers. In other words, the maximum consecutive natural number in the question can only be (x + 1) / 2. Let's call this number y.

Then we will try to find the consecutive numbers and add them as below:

```
1 + 2
  1 + 2 + 3
    // ...
    1 + 2 + 3 + ... + y
2 + 3
  2 + 3 + 4
    // ...
    2 + 3 + 4 +  ... + y
// ...
(y-1) + y
```

It is important to understand that there are two loops: the outside loop iterates which starting number; the inside loop decides how many consecutive numbers are used for adding.

Pseudocode

```
x   is the target number
for each number (starting_number) in 1 .. y-1
  for each number j in starting_number .. y
    calculate the sum (starting_number + 1) + (starting_number + 2) + ... + j
    if the sum is equal to x
      print out
    end
  end the internal loop
end loop
```

Purpose

- loop within another loop with different looping variables
- loop a number range with a variable
- print array element using a custom join character

Hints

We have done looping with a range before. For convenience, here is another example:

```
var x = 10
for i in 1...x-1 {
  print("\(i), ", terminator: "")
}
// will print 1, 2, 3, 4, 5, 6, 7, 8, 9,
```

To sum a range, we can convert a range to an array first, then use the standard array summing.

```
var array = Array(1...100)
Array(1...100).reduce(0, combine: +)   // => 5050
```

Join all elements of an array into a string

The code (extension method `combine`) below joins all items in an array into a string. This is often used for formatting array for display.

```swift
extension Array {
  func combine(separator: String) -> String{
    var str : String = ""
    for (idx, item) in enumerate(self) {
      str += "\(item)"
      if idx < self.count-1 {
          str += separator
      }
    }
    return str
  }
}

[1, 2, 3, 4].combine(separator: " + ") // => "1 + 2 + 3 + 4"
```

6.7 Exercises

Compute PI

Write a program to compute the value of Π based on the formula.

$$\pi = 4 \times (1 - \frac{1}{3} + \frac{1}{5} - \frac{1}{7} + \frac{1}{9} - \frac{1}{11} + \frac{1}{13} - \frac{1}{15} + ...)$$

Compute with different iteration count: 1, 100, 10000 and 1000000. Compare your result with Swift's built-in constant `Double.pi`. Your program shall look like:

```
Enter iteration count: 1
My computation PI = 4.0
  Swift's PI value: 3.141592653589793
```

7. Functions

With the solution in exercise 6.2 (finding the Highest Common Factor), we can see two code fragments (getting divisors for a number) that are almost identical, which is not optimal.

```
var divisorsList1: [Int] = []
var divisorsList2: [Int] = []

print("Enter first number: ")
var num1 = Int(readLine()!)
for x in 1...num1! {
  var check = num1! % x
  if check == 0 {
    divisorsList1.append(x)
  }
}

print("Enter second number: ")
var num2 = Int(readLine()!)
for x in 1...num2! {
  var check = num2! % x
  if check == 0 {
    divisorsList2.append(x)
  }
}
```

In programming, the functions removes duplication to make the code more readable, and most importantly, easy to maintain. A simple way of thinking the use of a function: a group of code statements that performs a task and can be reused.

A function consists of

1. **function name**. *What does it do?*
2. **parameters** (optional). *Input(s) passed to the function, the value of parameters are set by the callers, i.e. they change.*
3. **returned result**. *The result returned to the caller.*

Let's see an example function:

```
func add(a:Int, b:Int) -> Int {
  var c =  a + b
  return c
}
```

Where add is the function name, a and b are the two parameters and c is the result returned to the caller. In Swift, return ends the function.

Because Swift is a type safe language, every parameter and returned data type need to be declared. For example, the above add takes two integer parameters and returns an integer back. Type safety, checked at compile time, can prevent type errors (e.g. passing an Integer to aString by mistake).

The function names in Swift shall be starting with lowercase letters. For long function names using more than one word, the convention is to combine name with first character in up case with the exception of the first one, such as registerUser. It is a good idea to name your function that reveal its purpose well.

Here are two code statements calling the add function.

```
add(a: 1, b: 5)        // => 6
add(a: 100, b: 500)    // => 600
```

The above looks like some math functions such as $f(x) = x^2 - x + 1$. For example, a Swift function of this example math function might look like below:

```
func f(x:Int) -> Int {
  return x * x  - x + 1
}
```

7.1 Finding the Highest Common Factor (using function)

Write a program to ask the user to enter two non-negative integers and then find the highest common factor (HCF) of them. The program must define a function to return divisors of a number.

```
Enter the first number: (8)
Enter the second number: (12)
The HCF of 8 and 12 is: 4
```

Purpose

- Identify code duplication
- Remove duplication by introducing functions.

Hints

You may start with the existing solution of Exercise 6-4.

To define a function, ask the following 4 questions:

1. What does it do? (this helps to name it)
2. What shall I pass to the function?
3. What I expect to get back from this function?
4. How do I use the function?

```
func getDivisors(num: Int) -> [Int]{
  // ...
}

var divisorsList1 = getDivisors(num: 6)
var num2 = 10
var divisorsList2 = getDivisors(num: num2)

// ...
```

 ## Refactoring

The new code works the same way as our previous version, but it is better, right? The formal term to describe what you have just done in software programming is '**Code Refactoring**'. Code refactoring is the process of restructuring existing code - without changing its external behavior. To put in my simple words: "work the same outside, improved inside".

7.2 Generate Lotto Numbers (using a function)

Write a program to generate 6 Lotto numbers. Lotto numbers are between 1 and 49. This time, define a method that returns a valid lotto number.

```
Your winning lotto numbers are [23, 34, 12, 6, 7, 49], good luck!
```

Purpose

- move logic into functions to simplify the code
- refer variables outside the function scope

Analyze

This time, we use a function to simplify our code logic. Our target is to get 6 random numbers from 1 to 49. If we have a function that returns a random and not-appeared-before number, the solution is simple: calling the function 6 times.

Hints

```
var lottoNumbers: [Int] = []

func getNextValidLotteryNumber(existingNumbers: [Int])  -> Int {
  // randomly generate a number
  // check existing_lotto_numbers whether it appeared before
  // return one that satisfy, otherwise try again
}

newValidNumber = getNextValidLotteryNumber(existingNumbers: lottoNumbers)
lottoNumbers.append(newValidNumber)
```

7.3 Finding the LCM for multiple numbers (using function)

f()
12 18
 V
  6

Write a program to get the lowest number that is dividable by 1, 2, 3, 4, ..., 14 and 15.

```
The lowest number that is dividable by 1 to 15 is: 360360
```

Purpose

- Use the output of a function as a parameter to call the function again

Analyze

This is to calculate the LCM for multiple numbers. We have written a program to calculate the LCM for two numbers. If we divide 15 numbers into 15 calculations of LCM for two numbers, we get the answer.

```
1,     2 => LCM
LCM,   3 => LCM
LCM,   4 => LCM
...
LCM, 15 => LCM
```

Hints

You may start with the existing solution of Ex6-3, and refactor the code into a function.

```
func lcm(a: Int, b: Int) -> Int {
  // ...
}

lcm(a: 6, b: 8) // => 24
```

Then construct a loop to call this method based on our analysis.

8. File and Network

In previous exercises, we have collected data from user's input and printed output to the screen. In this chapter, we will write some programs to

- read from and write to files
- read data from Internet resources
- send emails

8.1 Calculate average score

Write a program that reads the contents of a text file containing scores of a class (0-100, one each line) and calculates the average score.

The content of the text file looks like the following:

```
84
78
...
87
```

The calculated average score is rounded to one decimal point.

```
> swift calc_average.swift
The average score is 79.8
```

Purpose

- Read text file into a string
- Read text file line by line
- Sum a list of integers

Analyze

The student scores are stored in a text file (the file content is in a text format, i.e. recognizable when opened in text editors. Image files such as JPEG are called binary files.

- read scores and process them
- sum and calculate the average

Hints

To work with a file, we must identify its path, e.g. '/Users/john/work/swiftcode/files/s-core.txt'. A file path is referred as a string.

To read all the content of a text file into a string.

```
let path:String = "/Users/john/work/swiftcode/files/score.txt"
let content = try String(contentsOfFile: path, encoding: NSUTF8StringEncoding)
print(content) // will print out full content
```

Process the file contents line by line.

```
let content = String(contentsOfFile: path, encoding: NSUTF8StringEncoding)
var strArray = content.componentsSeparatedByString("\n")

for line in strArray  {
  // process line
}
```

Relative Path

The paths start with "/" are called absolute paths. If a file is referenced this way and the program is running on another machine, it will fail as the referenced file does not exist. The safest way is to use relative path, i.e. the file path is relative to your program.

```
let bundle = NSBundle.mainBundle()
let path = bundle.pathForResource("score", ofType: "txt")
```

8.2 Count words and lines in a text file

WC	LC
21	3

Write a program that reads the contents of a file and counts the number of words and lines in that file.

```
swift count_words_lines.swift /Users/zhimin/work/swiftcode/files/novel.txt
'/Users/zhimin/work/swiftcode/files/novel.txt' contains 58611 words in 7898 lines
```

Purpose

- read command line arguments

Analyze

The program is a generic utility, which means we can use the program for different text files. Therefore, we cannot hardcode the input file path. When running a program from command line, we can pass arguments to the program. These arguments are called command line arguments.

Hints

Read command line arguments: `Process.arguments[]`

```
let firstCommandLineArgument = CommandLine.arguments[0] // the program
let secondCommandLineArgument = CommandLine.arguments[1]

print("Program: '\(firstCommandLineArgument)'")
print("The first argument is '\(secondCommandLineArgument)'")
```

The following batch command to run the above program in a Terminal window:

```
swift my_program.swift special.txt
```

will get output

```
Program: 'my_program.swift'
The first argument is 'special.txt'
```

For counting words (refer to chapter 4) and lines, you can use String's components method.

```
var wordCount = fileContent.components(separatedBy: CharacterSet.whitespaces).count
```

8.3 Mail merge birthday invitation cards

 Jessica is planning to invite her friends to her 12th birthday party. Instead of writing individual invitations, she wants to print them. Instead of creating documents one by one, she wants to generate a letter document (a text file) using the template below:

```
Dear {{first_name}},

I am celebrating my 12th Birthday on the 1st of April!
Come celebrate with me!

Where: 42 Greed-Island Street, Yorkshin City
When: 2PM to 5PM
RSVP: 24th March (0400-000-000 or rsvpjessica@gmail.com)

Hope to see you there,

Jessica.
```

Her friends: Pokkle, Angela, Tonpa, Toby, Biscuit, Mito, Kate, Renee, Chloe, Kelly and Melody.

Write a program to help Jessica generate multiple invitation cards as text files such as *pokkle_invitation.txt* and *angela_invitation.txt*.

Purpose

- Substitute text in a string
- Read text from text files
- Write content to text files

Analyze

This is a typical mail-merge type scenario: generating a set of documents. Each document has the same kind of information, some of the content is unique. We can create a template where parts of the document that can be substituted.

To perform a substitution, we need

- the section to be replaced in the template. For example, `{{first_name}}` is the one for this exercise.
- the text to replace into the template, i.e. friends' first names.

Once the text is substituted, it can be written into a text file.

Hints

Text Substitution

```
var str_1 = "We scare because we care"
var str_2 = str_1.replacingOccurrences(of: "scare", with: "laugh")
// => "We laugh because we care"
var str_3 = str_1.replacingOccurrences(of: "care", with: "cure")
// => "We scure because we cure"
```

`stringByReplacingOccurrencesOfString` replaces certain texts in a string and returns a modified string. It does not change the origin string.

```
var str_1 = "We scare because we care"
str_1.stringByReplacingOccurrencesOfString("we", withString: "he")
print(str_1);  // => not changed: "We scare because we care"
```

Write string to a text file

```
var newFileContent = "Laugh is the best medicine"
do {
  try new_file_content.writeToFile("/Users/zhimin/a_test_file.txt",
    atomically: false, encoding: NSUTF8StringEncoding)
} catch _ {
}
```

The first argument `/Users/zhimin/a_test_file.txt` is the path of the newly created file.

8.4 Rename files

 Write a program to rename the following files in a directory so that the files are always shown in alphabetical order and without spaces.

```
chapter 1.txt        chapter_01.txt
chapter 10.txt       chapter_02.txt
chapter 11.txt       chapter_03.txt
chapter 2.txt        chapter_04.txt
chapter 3.txt        chapter_05.txt
chapter 4.txt        chapter_06.txt
chapter 5.txt        chapter_07.txt
chapter 6.txt        chapter_08.txt
chapter 7.txt        chapter_09.txt
chapter 8.txt        chapter_10.txt
From chapter 9.txt   to  chapter_11.txt
```

(the directory with the above sample files can be found at *sources/files/book_dir*).

Purpose

- Process files in a directory
- Pattern matching using Regular Expression
- Rename files

Analyze

The objective is quite clear and can be divided in the following steps:

1. Iterate each file in a specified directory (by path)
2. Extract the number from the original file name, e.g. '9' from 'chapter 9.txt'
3. Construct a new file name, e.g. 'chapter_09.txt'
4. Rename the file

As you have mastered looping, it is a good idea to start with just renaming a single file. Once you have completed that, then process all the files in the directory.

Hints

Get files in a directory

```
let folderPath  = "\(NSHomeDirectory())/work/swiftcode/files/book_dir"

let fileManager = NSFileManager.defaultManager()
let enumerator:NSDirectoryEnumerator = fileManager.enumeratorAtPath(folderPath)!

while let fileName = enumerator.nextObject() as? String {
  // perform operation against fileName
}
```

Rename files

NSFileManager[1] defines a set of utility methods to manage files such as creating a new directory, copying and renaming files. `moveItemAtPath(_ srcPath: String,toPath dstPath: String)` method moves one file (by path), *renaming* is one form of 'moving'.

```
let fileManager = FileManager.default
var moveError: NSError?
do {
  try fileManager.moveItem(atPath: originFilePath, toPath: newFilePath)
} catch let error as NSError {
  moveError = error
  print(moveError!.localizedDescription)
}
```

Extract text using Regular Expression

Regular Expression (abbreviated *regex* or *regexp*) is a pattern of characters that finds matching text. Almost every programming languages support regular expression, with minor differences. A typical regular expression usage in Swift:

```
let regex = try! NSRegularExpression(pattern: "pattern", options: [])
```

Regular expression is very powerful and it does take some time to master it well. To get it going for simple text matching, however, is not hard. Google 'regular expression' shall return some good tutorials, and Rubular[2] is a helpful tool to let you try out regular expression online.

Here is an example regression expression for this program:

---

[1]https://developer.apple.com/library/ios/documentation/Cocoa/Reference/Foundation/Classes/NSFileManager_Class/
[2]http://rubular.com/

```
var fileName = "chapter 12.txt"
let regex = try! NSRegularExpression(pattern: "chapter\\s(\\d+)(.*)", options: [])
let matches = regex.matchesInString(fileName, options: [],
                range: NSRange(location: 0, length: fileName.utf16.count ))
let firstMatch = matches[0]
// range at index 0: full match
// range at index 1: first capture group
(fileName as NSString).substringWithRange(firstMatch.range(at: 1))  // => 12
(fileName as NSString).substringWithRange(firstMatch.range(at: 2))  // => .txt
```

where

- \d means to match a digit, 0 - 9
- \d+ matches 1 or more digits
- \s matches a white space character
- . matches any one character
- .* matches none or many any character
- () will pass matched text to special variables: $1 for first matched text, $2 for the second.

Adding leading zeros to a string

```
String(format: "%04d", 1)  // => "0001"
String(format: "%04d", 12) // => "0012"
```

8.5 Currency exchange with live quoting

$↔¥   Write a currency conversion program that converts Australian Dollars to Japanese Yen. To ensure we have a more accurate exchange rate, we will use Yahoo Finance's live currency rate service.

NOTE: Internet connection is required for this exercise.

```
Enter the amount of Australian dollars: 598
=> ¥ 56986.35
```

If you are unable to connect to Yahoo Finance (e.g. no internet connection), the program shall exit gracefully with an error message.

```
Unable to connect to Yahoo Finance,
Error: 'getaddrinfo: nodename nor servname provided, or not known'
```

Purpose

- Getting content from a URL

  Your program gets dynamic data from a URL and process it (you might have heard of a fancy name for this: Web Programming).
- Parse JSON string

  JSON stands for "JavaScript Object Notation", a very popular data format for exchanging data between software programs.

  ```
  {"AUD_JPY":{"val":81.163776}}
  ```
- Parse CSV

  CSV ("Comma Separated Values") file format is often used to exchange data in tabular form. Below is a sample CSV file:

  ```
  DESCRIPTION,LOGIN,PASSWORD,EXPECTED_TEXT
  Valid Login,agileway,test,Login Successful!
  User name not exists,nonexists,smartass,Login is not valid
  ```

  The easiest way to view CSV files is to open in Excel.
- Understanding API (Application Programming Interface) concept

  You can think API is the way for a software program to interact with another. The API for this currency change service is to provide live exchange rate in CSV format via HTTP protocol.
- Error handling

Analyze

As the requirement for this program is 'live exchange rate', we cannot use the hard-coded exchanges rates. In other words, the program shall use the current rate directly from the currency exchange market. You can see an example of live exchange rate between Australian dollar and Japanese Yen[3].

You may use one of the free exchange rate API below:

- Currency Converter API

  https://free.currencyconverterapi.com/api/v5/convert?q=AUD_JPY&compact=y
- Yahoo Finance API

  http://download.finance.yahoo.com/d/quotes.csv?s=AUDJPY=X&f=sl1d1t1ba&e=.csv

You can try it out by pasting the URL into your browser, you will see what you get back. Currency Converter API returns in JSON format; Yahoo Finance API returns CSV format.

Update: Yahoo Finance API is no longer accessible.

Hints

Get content from a URL

The Swift code below retrieves the exchange rate from a web address (called Uniform Resource Locator, URL in short).

```
let urlStr = "https://free.currencyconverterapi.com/api/v5/convert?q=AUD_JPY&compact=y"
var rateData : String = try! String(contentsOf: URL(string: myURLString)!,
                                    encoding: String.Encoding.utf8)
```

Exception handling

The above code only works if you are connected to Internet and exchange rate server is up running. If not, you will get an error message like below:

```
fatal error: 'try!' expression unexpectedly raised an error: Error Domain=
NSURLErrorDomain Code=-1003 "A server with the specified hostname could not be found."
```

This brings an important concept in programming: Exception handling. An exception means an anomalous or exceptional condition occurred. The code to handle exceptions is called exception handling. If an exception is not handled, the program execution will terminate with the exception displayed. Here is the exception handling syntax in Swift:

---

[3]https://au.finance.yahoo.com/q?s=AUDJPY=X

```
do {
    try expression
} catch {
    // handle when exception occurs
}
```

Let's look at an example.

```
var s : String?
let myURLString = "http://abc.clinicwise.net"
do {
  s = try! String(contentsOf: URL(string: myURLString)!, encoding: String.Encoding.utf8)
} catch let error as NSError{
  print("Error occurred: \(error)")
}
```

During the execution, an exception is raised and then handled. Here is the output:

```
Error occurred: Error Domain=NSCocoaErrorDomain Code=260 "The file couldn't be opened ..."
The code can still continue
```

Parse exchange rate in JSON from currencyconverterapi.com

Swift 4 introduces basic support (in my view) for JSON.

```
let rateJSONData; // a String contains rates in format of '{"AUD_JPY":{"val":81.163776}}'
let decoder = JSONDecoder()
let decodedJson: [String: [String: Double]] = try! decoder.decode(
      [String: [String: Double]].self, from: rateJSONData.data(using: .utf8)!)
let theRate = decodedJson["AUD_JPY"]!["val"]!
```

Read CSV

Swift does not have built-in support for CSV, the below is a very rudimentary way to parse one line CSV (good for this exercise) using `String.componentsSeparatedByString()` method to split a CSV string to an array based on the comma delimiter.

```
//rateCsvData from Yahoo Finance:  "AUDJPY=X",88.0985,"1/1/2016","11:11pm",87.6432,88.5537
let csvParagraphs = rateCsvData.components(separatedBy: ",")
let exchangeRate = Double(csvParagraphs[1] as String)!
```

Code is for computers as well as Human

While the code is for machines to execute, don't forget its another important audience: human being. Software requires regular updates and being maintained, you and fellow programmers will need to understand and modify the code some time later. By then, well written code will make future work easier, more importantly, reduce the chance of introducing defects. This might take years to master, but I would suggest developing habits to put some thoughts for code quality when programming.

8.6 Exercises

GradesHistogram

Write a program that reads grades (between 0 and 100, integer) from a text file and display the histogram.

For example:

```
49 50 51 59 0 5 9 10 15 19 50 68 55 89 100 99
```

Output:

```
 0 -  9: ***
10 - 19: ***
20 - 29:
30 - 39:
40 - 49: *
50 - 59: *****
60 - 69: *
70 - 79:
80 - 89: *
90 -100: **
```

9. Object Oriented Programming

Swift is an object-oriented programming language. Please bear with me if you have no idea what object-oriented is.

I remember that it took me quite a while to understand object-oriented concept when I was at university back in early 90s. I had no tools to try, just read theories from books. It turned out to be quite simple if it was illustrated with examples. Here is one:

Car is a class, a type of something, it has following two functions (plus many more...):

- accelerate
- brake

My car (the one in my garage) is an object of Car, it can do 'brake' and 'accelerate'. I can physically drive it.

Now have a think about statements below:

```
my_car = Car()
my_car.accelerate()
your_camry = Car()
your_camry.brake()
```

You may recall some code we have used:

```
var product = "iPad"
product.hasPrefix("i")    // => true
var iphones = ["iPhone 4s", "iPhone 5S", "iPhone 5C"]
iphones.sort{ $0 < $1 }    // =>["iPhone 4s", "iPhone 5C", "iPhone 5S"]
```

product is an object of class String, and iphones is an object of class Array. Here is how to find out an object's class.

```
_stdlib_getDemangledTypeName(product)  // => "Swift.String"
_stdlib_getDemangledTypeName(iphones)  // => "Swift.Array"
```

The reason we are able to call .hasPrefix and .sort is because these methods are defined in the String and Array classes respectively.

Most modern programming languages support Object-oriented programming (OOP). Mastering OOP is a must for programmers nowadays.

9.1 Calculator (Class)

Write a Calculator class that contains two methods:

- Add two numbers
- Subtract two numbers

```
print( calc.add(one: 2, another: 3) )   // => 5
print( calc.minus(one: 17, another: calc.add(one: 2, another:3) ) )  // => 12
```

Purpose

- Define a class
- Define methods in a class
- Create a new instance (object) of a class
- Invoke a method on an object

Analyze

This program is quite easy if using standard methods (Chapter 7). The purpose of this exercise is to do it in a class, object-oriented way. If you understand the basic Swift Class syntax and usage (see below), this exercise is quite straightforward.

Hints

define a class

A Swift Class name needs to in capital case, for example, "BankAccount".

```
class BankAccount  {

  // ...

}
```

define functions in a class

The definition of methods in classes are the same as standard methods (Chapter 7), except that they are within the scope of a class. To put simply, the methods in a class are only available to its objects.

```
class BankAccount  {

  func transfer(amount: Float, anotherAccount: BankAccount) {
    // ...
  }

}
```

create objects using *new* method

Objects are instances of the class.

```
// BankAccount class is already defined
savingAccount = BankAccount()
chequeAccount = BankAccount()
```

invoke an object's method

```
savingAccount.transfer(amount: 100, anotherAccount: chequeAccount)
```

9.2 Age of Teacher and Students

 A school consists of teachers and students, and students are grouped by grades. Write a program to calculate

- a teacher's age
- the average age of teachers
- the average age of Grade 10 students

```
var teacher_1 = Teacher(name: "James Bond", birthDate: "1968-04-03")
var teacher_2 = Teacher(name: "Michael Zasky", birthDate: "1978-01-02")

var students = [Student]()
students.append(Student(name: "John Sully", birthDate: "1999-10-03",  grade:10))
students.append(Student(name: "Michael Page", birthDate: "1999-05-07", grade:11))
students.append(Student(name: "Anna Boyle", birthDate: "1998-12-03",  grade:10))
students.append(Student(name: "Dominic Chan", birthDate: "1999-09-10", grade:10))
```

Output:

```
Teacher 'James Bond' age: 46
Average Teacher age: 41.0
The number of Grade 10 students: 3
Average Grade 10 students age: 15.0
```

Purpose

- Instance variables
- Read and write instance variables
- Class Constructor
- Class Inheritance
- Age calculation
- Use of array operations (review)

Analyze

The core function is to calculate ages, and we have two identified Classes Teacher and Student (from the code fragment). We could write two get_age functions in both Teacher and Student classes, however this is not correct. You wouldn't want to write another get_age method to support another class AdminStaff.

Calculating ages (from birth date) is a common function for human. In OOP, we can move common methods into its parent class, then its child classes inherit them. This is called "Inheritance" (see hints below). For this exercise, we can create another class Person with age method, then make Teacher and Student inherit from Person. Here is the class diagram for the design.

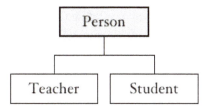

After deciding the class design at high level, we turn to Class internals. Each teacher or student has name and 'birthdate (needed for calculating the age). Student also shall have a grade'. These are attributes of a Class, also known as "class instance variables" (see hints below).

Let me illustrate with an example:

```
John Sully is a 10 Grade student, he was born in 1999-10-23
James Bond is a teacher, born in 1968-04-03
```

The information can be represented in this code:

```
var john_sully = Student(name: "John Sully", birthDate: "1999-10-23", grade: 10)
var james_bond = Teacher(name: "James Bond", birthDate: "1968-04-03")
```

where john_sully is an object (or instance) of class Student and james_bond is an object of class Teacher. The data in brackets were stored in each object's attributes.

```
john_sully.grade  // => 10
james_bond.name   // => "James Bond"
```

The business function of this exercise is to calculate age from birth date. We all know how to do it: comparing the birth date against today's date. However, this can be a bit tricky. See hints for how to use Swift's built-in date helper methods.

Hints

Class Constructor

Calling `class()` creates an object of the class. There is a special method inside Class to respond to this operation: `init`. This method is also called "Constructor". Except its special meaning (returning a new object) and predefined method name `init`, the syntax of a constructor is pretty much like a method.

```
class Person {

  var name: String

  init(name: String) {
    self.name = name
  }

}
```

The code below creates two `Person` objects.

```
var john_smith = Person(name: "John Smith")
var mary_boyle = Person(name: "Mary Boyle")
```

Class instance properties

A Class usually has certain properties (also called attributes), such as "Person has name, birth date, ...". These properties are declared directly under `class Name {`.

```
class Person {

  var name: String
  var gender: String?   // optional, allowing nil
  var age: Int = Int()  // initialized with value : 0

  init(name: String) {
    self.name = name  // self.name is the property, name is parameter
  }

}
```

All properties shall be initialized (in `init()`) unless it is specified to be optional as in `var gender: String?`. Taking out the ? will throw an error.

```
error: return from initializer without initializing all stored properties
```

The value of a property in each class instance can be set differently.

```
var bruce = Person(name: "Bruce Lee")
bruce.age   // => 0
bruce.age = 32
bruce.gender  = "Male"
print("\(bruce.name)'s age is \(bruce.age)")
// output: "Bruce Lee's age is 32"
var jackie = Person(name: "Jackie Chan")
jackie.age = 61
```

Class Inheritance

Inheritance is a relation between two classes. For example, seagulls and parrots are both birds, thus they share the common features of birds.

```
class Bird {
  init() { }
  func fly() {
    print("I am flying")
  }
}

class Seagull : Bird {
}

class Parrot : Bird {
```

```
  func speak() {
    print("if someone teaches me")
  }
}

var seagull = Seagull()
seagull.fly()    // => "I am flying"

var parrot = Parrot()
parrot.fly()     // => "I am flying"
parrot.speak()   // => "if someone teaches me"

seagull.speak() // Error: 'Seagull' does not have a member named `speak'
```

By using inheritance, the code (defined in methods) can be reused.

Override methods

Child classes may override its parent behaviour by supplying new implementation: defining the same method with different statements inside.

```
class Ostrich : Bird {
  override func fly() {
    print("I'd rather run")
  }
}

var ostrich = Ostrich()
ostrich.fly() // => "I'd rather run"
```

Parse date string to a NSDate object

Commonly, we start with a date string (user entered), to convert a NSDate object:

```
var aDate:String = "2006-12-15"
let dateFormatter = NSDateFormatter()
dateFormatter.dateFormat = "YYYY-MM-DD"
var birthDate = dateFormatter.dateFromString(aDate)
```

Date calculation

User NSCalendar to calculate the differences between two dates, for a person's age in this case. NSDate() returns current time.

```
func age(birthDate: NSDate) -> Int {
  let calendar  = NSCalendar.currentCalendar();
  let ageComponents = calendar.components(.Year,
      fromDate: birthDate,
      toDate: NSDate(),
      options: [])

  return ageComponents.year
}
```

9.3 Calculate Sales Tax

10%
GST

The sales tax in Australia is called Goods and services tax (GST) of 10%, which is applied to most products and services. For example, in a physio clinic, medical services such as physiotherapy is GST-free, however GST applies to pilates classes (also a service), so is to all products sold at the clinic. All business must show "GST-inclusive prices". For example, for a $10 meal, $9.09 is net amount and $0.91 is sales tax.

Complete the program below to calculate the net amount and sales tax of product and services.

```
// ... define Class Goods and ServiceItem

var foam_roller = Goods(name: "Foam Roller", amount: 49.95);
var physio_service = ServiceItem(name: "Physio Consultation", amount: 120.0);
var pilates_class = ServiceItem(name: "Pilates Classes", amount: 80.0)
pilates_class.sales_tax_applicable = true
// ... statements to print out product and services' net amount and sale tax
```

Output:

```
Foam Roller Net Amount: 45.41, GST: 4.54
Physio Consultation Net Amount: 120.0, GST: 0.0
Pilates Classes Net Amount: 72.73, GST: 7.27
```

Purpose

- Class Design
- Protocol Extensions
- Class Constructor setting default value of instance variables

Analyze

From the given code fragment, two classes Goods and ServiceItem need to be defined. The sales tax calculation code is shared between the two classes. There are two common approaches to achieve code reuse:

- Inheritance

- Protocol Extensions

We have used 'Inheritance' in the previous exercises. Here we will be using 'Protocol Extensions'. "A protocol defines a blueprint of methods, properties, and other requirements that suit a particular task or piece of functionality". It is similar to Interface in Java or C#.

Here is an example protocol extension for logging (print out in a formatted way, typically to a file).

```
protocol Loggable {
  func log(message: String)
}

// default implementation
extension Loggable {
  func log(message: String) {
    print( "[\(NSDate())] [\(_stdlib_getDemangledTypeName(self))] \(message)");
  }
}
```

To utilize the logging, we need to make the class to implement Loggable protocol.

```
class A : Loggable {
}

class B : Loggable {

}

class C  {
}

var a = A()
var b = B()
var c = C()

a.log("in A") // => [2016-01-01 16:07:32 +1000] [A] in A
b.log("in B") // => [2016-01-01 16:07:32 +1000] [B] in B
c.log("in C") // => error: value of type 'C' has no member 'log'
```

c.log() failed because the class c did not include the Logging module, therefore the method log is not available. Please note that output the log message printed out class names dynamically based on which class it is called from.

You may wonder, why bother `Protocol Extensions`? Let's examine the above example again, how will you do it differently? Logging is a common function in many different classes, we don't want to duplicating `log()` method in each class and inheritance does not fit well. Swift does not support multiple class inheritance, but a class may implement multiple protocols. By using protocol extensions, we may provide the same protocol implementation across different classes, i.e. achieving code reuse.

Hints

 The concept of Protocol Extensions can be quite confusing to beginners. I would recommend start writing the program first in the standard Object Oriented way:

- Design the Classes first
- Identify their attributes
- Identify their methods
- Implement the methods

Then try to introduce Protocol Extensions to optimize the program: remove the code duplication.

Setting default value to instance variables in the constructor

Quite common, the value of certain instance variables are the same for most cases. Instead of an parameter in the class constructor, we could set the default value. If necessary, we can change its value via a setter method (`object.attr = `).

```
class Student {
  var name:String
  var isTalented:Bool

  init(name: String) {
    self.name = name
    self.isTalented = false // defualt to false
  }
}

var john = Student(name: "John Smith")
john.isTalented    // => false

var newton = Student(name: "Newton")
```

```
newton.isTalented = true
newton.isTalented    // => true
```

Protocol Extensions : Taxable

```
protocol Taxable {

  var amount: Double { get set }
  var sales_tax_applicable: Bool { get set }

  func netAmount() -> Double   // no implementation
  func gst() -> Double            // no implementation
}
```

As you can see, it is quite similar to `Class` in terms of syntax and structure.

```
Extension

extension Taxable {

  func netAmount() -> Double {
    // ...
  }

  func gst() -> Double {
    // ...
  }

}
```

9.4 Library System

Implement a simplified library system. Initially, the librarian can import book records into the system via a CSV file. Members of the library can borrow and return books.

```
let booksCsvFile  = "\(NSHomeDirectory())/work/swiftcode/files/books.csv"
Library.importBooks(booksCsvFile)
Library.bookCount() // => 10
```

The format of CSV file:

```
TITLE, AUTHOR
The 4-Hour Workweek, Timothy Ferriss
How to Win Friends and Influence People, Dale Carnegie
```

Here is an example use of the library system:

```
var john = Member(name: "John Sully", memberId: "1001")
var mike = Member(name: "Mike Zasky", memberId: "1002")

var book = Library.findByTitle("Practical Web Test Automation")
Library.borrow(john, book!)
// Output "OK"
Library.borrow(mike, book!)
// Output: The book 'Practical Web Test Automation' is not available!
Library.return(book)
Library.borrow(mike, book!)
// Output "OK"
```

Purpose

- Class Methods
- Class Variables
- Class Design
- Load CSV data into objects
- Find matching objects in an array

Analyze

By examining the nouns in the description of this exercise, we can identify 3 classes:

- **Book**

  Book has two attributes: *title* and *author*.
- **Member**

  Member has two attributes: *name* and *memberId*.
- **Library**

  The main class for this exercise. Library members belong to the library, so are the books. So `Library` has to attributes: *books* and *members*. Because there will one instance of `Library`, we don't need to create an instance, just use `Library` class. `books` and `members` are class variables (see hints below) of `Library`.

  `borrow`, `returnBook` and `findByTitle` are `Library`'s class methods.

Not all classes can be directly extracted from the problem description. For example, book lending is associated to records, a `Rental` class.

- **Rental**

  borrowing records containing the member and the book information.

Hints

Class Variables and Class Methods

In comparison to instance variables, class variables are shared by all instances of a Class. Let me illustrate with an example,

- john's car is Honda Accord
- mike's car is Toyota Camry

Both cars are Sedan, I can represent this in Swift Class:

```
class Sedan {
  var make: String
  var model: String

  init(make: String, model: String) {
    self.make = make
    self.model = model
  }

}

var johns_car = Sedan(make: "Honda", model: "Accord")
var mikes_car = Sedan(make: "Toyota", model: "Camry")
```

Obviously, the make and model are instance variables, as different objects may have different values. Now, if I ask you how many wheels does John's car or Mike's car have? The answer is 4. In fact, 4 is the answer to all sedans.

```
class Sedan {
  static var numWheels:Int = 4
}

Sedan.numWheels  // => 4
```

Class variables are called static variables in Swift. The numWheels is a static variable of Sedan.

Library's static variables

```
class Library {
  // Book, Member, Rental classes already defined
  static var books:     [Book] = []
  static var members: [Member] = []
  static var rentals: [Rental] = []

  // ...
}
```

Library's Class Methods

```
class Library {

  class func importBooks(csv_file: String) {
    //  read CSV and create book objects (see the hint below)
  }

  class func borrow(member: Member, book: Book) {
    //  create rental object
    //  update book status
  }

  // and more ...
}
```

A checked out book is not available to borrow, have a think about how to ensure that.

Load CSV data into objects

Parse the CSV file (we covered CSV in Chapter 8), then create objects from the data.

```
var fileContent = ""
do {
  fileContent = try String(contentsOfFile: csvFilePath, encoding: NSUTF8StringEncoding)
} catch let error as NSError {
  print("Error: \(error)")
}

var lines = fileContent.componentsSeparatedByString("\n")
for var line in lines {
  var fields = line.componentsSeparatedByString(",")
  if fields.count < 2 || fields[0] == "TITLE" { // empty file or heading row
    continue
  }
  books.append( Book(title: fields[0], author: fields[1]) )
}
```

Find matching objects in an array

```
class func findByTitle(book_title: String) -> Book? {
  var the_book: Book?
  for book in books {
    if book.title == book_title {
      the_book = book
      break
    }
  }
  print("Book '\(book_title)' not found")
  return the_book
}
```

9.5 Sunflower vs Zombies Game Simulation

 This is a simplified simulation of the famous "Plants vs Zombies" Game. A sunflower is on the left of the field, zombies come towards the flower (to eat it) one by one. The purpose of the game is to let the flower to survive one wave of attack (15 zombies).

Each step a zombie makes, there will be "exchange of fire" (the sunflower shoots seeds to the zombie; the zombie throws stones to the sunflower), both the flower and the zombie receive a certain degree of damage to their health. If the attacking zombie's health down to 0%, the zombie dies and then comes another until no more. If the sunflower's health reaches 0%, game over.

Game rules:

- The health level of the sunflower and zombies start at 100%
- Zombie needs to travel 10 steps to get to the sunflower
- During 'exchange of fire', the damage to the zombie and the sunflower are nondeterministic. The flower receives a lot less damage than the zombie.
- If a zombie arrives next to the sunflower, it will cause bigger damage to the sunflower.
- There is a rare specie of Jump Zombie who can move two steps at a time.
- The game speed is adjustable.

User Interface (UI) requirement:

This simulation is dynamically presented in text (not graphic), the zombies and the sunflower are represented as Z(health) and F(health) respectively. The movement of zombies is indicated by placing the zombie in the field as below.

```
F(100)   ___ ___ ___ ___ ___ ___ ___ ___ ___ Z87
F( 98)   ___ ___ ___ ___ ___ ___ ___ ___ Z38 ___
F( 95)   ___ ___ ___ ___ ___ ___ ___ Z00 ___ ___
```

While the above show 3 lines of printed out text, in the simulation, there shall be only one (see hints). The line text is re-printed again and again to achieve a "Motion" effect.

if the sunflower wins,

```
F( 11)   ___ ___ ___ ___ ___ ___ ___ Z00 ___ ___
```

```
You Win! Flower survived attacks from 15 zombies.
```

if the zombies win,

```
F(  0)   ___ ___ ___ ___ ___ ___ Z18 ___ ___ ___
```

```
Game Over! 2 zombies left.
```

Purpose

- Game Design
- Use of Class Variables and Class Methods
- Overwrite previously printed line

Analyze

This program is quite complex, as always, it is a good idea to start with class design.

Clearly, we have two classes: Flower and Zombie. There are one Flower instance and 15 Zombie instances. The health attributes of both classes are used to determine live or death of an object.

The distance a zombie has travelled (step) can be used for determining whether to apply "close-combat damage". Jump Zombie moves 2 steps at one go, so there should be a movingSpeed attribute. To simulate randomness of Jump Zombies appearing, we can set a higher movingSpeed value based on probability when creating a zombie instance.

After defined the attributes, we move on to the methods (or behaviours).

Flower

- *exchange_fire*: called when a zombie move forward a step. This records the damage to the sunflower and the only zombie in the field. We can add randomness there to increase unpredictability of simulation.
- *die*: health down to 0%.

Zombie

- *move_forward*: move one or two steps based on the object's speed.

- *die*: health down to 0%.

We can also add some helper methods such as `is_dead?`, `in_touch_distance?`.

With the class design completed, we move to the game engine. The game is running as long as the sunflower is alive and there are zombies remaining. A typical `while` loop here. Within each loop,

- check and locate the next zombie. End game if no more.
- the active zombie move forward a step (or two steps if is a Jumpy) and exchange fire with the sunflower.
- print out the "battle scene"

Hints

CONSTANTS

A constant is like a variable, except that its value is supposed to remain constant for the duration of the program. A Swift constant's name starts with an upper case letter, commonly all upper cases.

```
let ZOMBIES_COUNT = 15
```

If you later change the value of a constant later, Swift will throw an error.

```
// ...
ZOMBIES_COUNT = 10 // error: cannot assign to value: 'ZOMBIES_COUNT'
// is a 'let' constant, note: change 'let' to 'var' to make it mutable
```

Using static variables in the game

Swift supports static variables in classes. This is not exactly the same as a class variable as they aren't inherited by subclasses).

```
class Zombie {
  static var liveCount :Int = 0

  init() {
    // ...
    Zombie.liveCount += 1
  }

}

var zombies = [Zombie]()
zombies.append(Zombie()) // add one
zombies.append(Zombie()) // add another
print(Zombie.liveCount)  // => 2
```

Create Jump Zombies

```
var movingSpeed: Int

  init() {
    //...
    movingSpeed = (random() % 10) >= 8  ?  2 : 1  // 20% are jumping zombies
  }
```

movingSpeed is used in move_forward() function to reflect a zombie's traveling pace.

Overwrite previously printed line

We used print a lot, which prints out text and a new line. To just print out text, use
print("text", terminator: "").

```
print("Good")
print("Morning")
print("See ", terminator: "")
print("You", terminator: "")
print("Later", terminator: "")
```

Output:

```
Good
Morning
See YouLater
```

To overwrite previously printed line, add \r (carriage return without a line feed).

```
print("First Line", terminator: "")
fflush(__stdoutp) // flush stdout to see the text immediately
sleep(2)  // to see "First Line" displayed briefly
// ... no other print statements
print("\rSecond Line")
```

Running the code in a console, the final output will be only "Second Line" after showing 'First Line' briefly. You don't get this effect in Xcode output window.

9.6 Exercises

Calculate Shape Area

Define four classes: Shape, Rectangle, Triangle and Square. Define area method and attributes in these classes to calculate the shape area. The usage like below:

```
puts Triangle.new(10, 5).area()
puts Rectangle.new(10, 5).area()
puts Square.new(10).area()
```

Try using Class Inheritance as possible.

Hints

Draw a diagram like the one in Exercise 9.2 first.

10. Classic Puzzles

In this chapter, we will use our coding skills to solve some fun puzzles. You might have seen them before, but solving it with code will be more interesting.

10.1 Google Labs Aptitude Test

Solve this cryptic equation, every letter represent a distinct number between 0 - 9. No leading zeros are allowed. (This was a Google Interview question).

```
    WWWDOT
  - GOOGLE
  --------
    DOTCOM
```

Purpose

- Using nested loops
- Trying with unique numbers within nested loops

Analyze

We have 9 letters here.

```
W D O T G L E C M
```

W, G and D cannot be 0.

A brute-force way is to try every combination of 26 alphabetic characters using fast computing computer of the computers:

- W = 1, D = 0, O = 0, T = 0, G = 0, L = 0, E = 0, C = 0, M = 0

- W = 1, D = 0, O = 0, T = 0, G = 0, L = 0, E = 0, C = 0, M = 1
- W = 1, D = 0, O = 0, T = 0, G = 0, L = 0, E = 0, C = 0, M = 2
- ...
- W = 1, D = 0, O = 0, T = 0, G = 0, L = 0, E = 0, C = 0, M = 9
- W = 1, D = 0, O = 0, T = 0, G = 0, L = 0, E = 0, C = 1, M = 0

..., until find a solution.

We all know that this is not efficient. However, a simple solution utilising computing power (otherwise idle) is not bad sometimes.

For these 9 letters, each represents a unique digit (0-9). Brute force method means trying 1 - 9 for W, within this loop, trying 0-9 for 'D' until to the 9th letter M. The core logic is within the most inner loop:

- construct the top number (WWWDOT)
- construct the bottom number (GOOGLE)
- construct the result (DOTCOM)
- print out the solution if the top number minus the bottom number is equal to the result

A brute force approach usually takes quite a while to solve, due to a large number of looping. It is important to add constraints to reduce the number of loops (the code checking the calculation). For example, by adding checking for uniqueness (if W is 1, D cannot be 1, O cannot be equal to W and D, ..., etc), the number of effective loops is reduced to 2,540,160, from possible 729,000,000!

Hints

Nested Loops

The code below prints a 9x9 times table.

```
for i in 1...9 {
  for j in 1...9 {
    print( "\(i) x \(j) = \(i*j)")
  }
}
```

Output:

```
1 x 1 = 1
1 x 2 = 2
1 x 3 = 3
1 x 4 = 4
1 x 5 = 5
1 x 6 = 6
1 x 7 = 7
1 x 8 = 8
1 x 9 = 9
2 x 1 = 2
2 x 2 = 4
...
9 x 9 = 81
```

Construct number from digits

```
var a = 3
var b = 6
var c = 5
var numDays = a * 100 + b * 10 + c  // => 365
```

10.2 Fibonacci and HCF (Recursion)

 We have done the Fibonacci exercise before. This time, we will use Recursion. Before I explain what is Recursion, let's examine the formula of Nth Fibonacci number:

```
fib(1) = 1
fib(2) = 1
fib(n) = fib(n-1) + fib(n-2)
```

If I asked "what is the 6th fibonacci number?", many can answer quickly. What if I change the question to 674th Fibonacci number? By now, I hope you have developed the habit of "thinking" like a computer. Back to the question, have a look at this worksheet.

fib(6) = fib(5) + fib(4)   fib(6) = 5 + 3 = 8

    fib(5) = fib(4) + fib(3)   fib(5) = 3 + 2 = 5

       fib(4) = fib(3) + fib(2)   fib(4) = 2 + 1 = 3

          fib(3) = fib(2) + fib(1)   fib(3) = 1 + 1 = 2

fib(2) =1, fib(1) = 1

As you see, we don't know the answer to fib(6), fib(5) and fib(4). Until we reach `fib(3)` = `fib(2)` + `fib(1)`, as `fib(2)` and `fib(1)` are known. Then we use the result to work backwards to get fib(4), fib(5) and fib(6). This is a Recursion method.

Recursion refers to a method which solves a problem by solving a smaller version of the problem and then using that result to work out the answer to the original problem. In the context of programming, **a recursive method calls itself**. This might seem complex and hard to comprehend. If we change the thinking angle, it actually can be quite natural to certain problems.

Recursion can only be a applied to certain problems; where the problem (usually in a form of a formula) can be broken into smaller problems, like Fibonacci. Here is a solution to Fibonacci:

```
func fibonacci(num:Int) -> Int {
  if (num <= 1) {
    return num
  }
  return fibonacci(num: num - 1) + fibonacci(num: num - 2)
}
print( fibonacci(num: 10) )  // => 55
```

The code is quite concise, isn't it? Let's examine this code.

1. **Method definition with parameters**.

   `func fibonacci(num)` is a normal method, but it is called twice within the method self. The parameters of a recursion method is important.

2. **End cause**.

   Without that, a method calling itself will lead to an infinite loop. `if (num <= 1) {;` `return n; }` means if the parameter `num` is less than or equal to 1, the call returns a result back. This only ends the current method call, its result will be returned to other recursive method calls that have been waiting.

3. **Calculation with calling itself**.

   The core logic is based on the identified formula.

Try using recursion to solve Highest Common Factor (HCF) problem with Euclidean algorithm[1], a much more efficient way. The algorithm:

```
hcf(a, 0) = a
hcf(a, b) = hcf(b, a mod b)
```

Hints

Math Mod

The remainder of a division.

```
10 % 4  // => 2
```

---

[1]http://en.wikipedia.org/wiki/Greatest_common_divisor#Using_Euclid.27s_algorithm

10.3 Calculate Compound Interest

 We earn interest on the money deposited in the bank. The interest we receive for the first year will be added to the principal (and then calculate the interest for the next year), this is called Compound Interest. Write a program to calculate how much money you will receive back at the given rate after certain years.

```
Enter deposited amount : $10000
Enter interest rate (8% enter 0.08): 0.06
For how long (years): 12

After 12 years, you will get $20121.96
```

Purpose

- Recursion
- Review reading user input and printing formatted output

Analyze

Calculating compound interest, maybe less obvious than Fibonacci sequence, can be be solved with recursion. The essence of the compound interest is that the principal (money we deposit in the bank) plus the interest of the year becomes the new principal for the next year.

```
total_money_back(year) = total_money_back(year-1) + interest_amount
```

Hints

Make effective use of parameters of a recursion method.

```
// ...
var totalAmount = compoundInterest(principal: amount, rate: rate, years: years)
```

Recursion

```
var newPrincipal = principal + rate * principal // new principal for this year
compoundInterest(principal: newPrincipal, rate: rate, years: years-1)
```

Rule of 72 for estimating compound interest

A quicker way to find out the number of years requires to double your money at a given interest rate: Divide the interest rate into 72. For example, if the interest rate is 8%, 72 / 8 ⇒ 9 years.

Verify Rule of 72 with your program.

10.4 Farmer Crosses River Puzzle

 A farmer wants to cross a river and take with him a wolf, a goat, and a cabbage. There is a boat that can fit himself plus either the wolf, the goat, or the cabbage. If the wolf and the goat are alone on one shore, the wolf will eat the goat. If the goat and the cabbage are alone on the shore, the goat will eat the cabbage.

How can the farmer bring the wolf, the goat, and the cabbage across the river?

```
Step 0
[] <= [:farmer, :wolf, :sheep, :cabbage]
Step 1 [:farmer, :sheep] forward
[:farmer, :sheep] <= [:wolf, :cabbage]
Step 2 [:farmer] backward
[:sheep] <= [:farmer, :wolf, :cabbage]
Step 3 [:farmer, :wolf] forward
[:farmer, :wolf, :sheep] <= [:cabbage]
Step 4 [:farmer, :sheep] backward
[:wolf] <= [:farmer, :sheep, :cabbage]
Step 5 [:farmer, :cabbage] forward
[:farmer, :wolf, :cabbage] <= [:sheep]
Step 6 [:farmer] backward
[:wolf, :cabbage] <= [:farmer, :sheep]
Step 7 [:farmer, :sheep] forward
[:farmer, :wolf, :sheep, :cabbage] <= []
Done!
```

Purpose

- Backtracking algorithm

Analyze

Remember your first attempts on this famous puzzle, maybe like this:

1. Choose farmer and over the river, oops, back.
2. Choose farmer and sheep over the river, check, good.
   1. farmer back, still good.

      2. farmer and cabbage cross, OK.

      3. farmer back, oops, back.

  3. ...

This trial and error method is called backtracking in programming. Backtracking is an algorithmic paradigm that tries different possibilities until a solution is found.

```
make_a_move {

  if all crossed river? {
    print out all moves
    exit
  }

  for each four items including the farmer {

    move the item with the farmer, if item is farmer just move him

    if is_safe? and has_not_done_this_move_before? {
      make_a_move // recursive
    } else {
      undo_the_move
    }
  }
}
```

End cause

All three items and the farmer crossed the river.

Constraints

1. Farmer does not cross river empty handed as there is no point of doing that. He can come back empty handed though.
2. The item to be moved has to be on the same side with the farmer
3. Safety check
   - sheep and cabbage cannot be on the same side without the farmer
   - wolf and sheep cannot be on the same side without the farmer
4. The move has not been done before

Hints

Data Design

> "Algorithms + Data Structures = Programs" is a famous book by Niklaus Wirth, published in 1976.

For a complex program, it is important to design the data structure at first. Data structure is how the data is organized and stored in the program; Algorithm is how a program to solve a program, using the data.

Besides simple data types (such as Integer and String), we have used the following composite types:

- Array
- Dictionary
- Class

For this puzzle, the data structures are relatively simple.

```
var itemPositions = ["farmer": "not_crossed", "wolf": "not_crossed", "sheep": "not_crosse\
d", "cabbage": "not_crossed" ]
let items = ["farmer", "wolf", "sheep", "cabbage"]
var direction = "forward"  // default, another value "backward"
```

I used instance variables @xxx here. As this is a quite complex program, several methods will be used. By using instance variables, I can use them in any methods without worrying about the scopes.

Once the data is defined, it is not hard to write the following methods:

- check whether all items are crossed?

  ```
  func isAllCrossedRiver() -> Bool {
    // check for itemPositions
  }
  ```
- is safe to cross?

```
func isSafe() -> Bool {
  // check itemPositions, both sides!
end
```

- is the item with the farmer?

```
func isItemWithFarmer(item: String) -> Bool  {
    // check itemPositions
}
```

- move one item (with or just the farmer)

```
func move(item: String) {
  // change value for the item and the farmer in itemPositions
  // toggle direction
}
```

- undo the previous move as it does not satisfy the constraints

```
func undoMove(item: String)  {
  // revert value for the item and the farmer in itemPositions
  // toggle direction
}
```

Store moving log

We need to keep a record of every movement made so that we can print out the solution.

```
// moving log starts with all in one side
var movingLog = [ 0: itemPositions ];
```

The above statement stores the step number and the items position in a hash. dup stands for 'duplicate'; this creates a copy of the object so that the original object won't be affected by changes.

For every move, we add it to the movingLog. When reaching the solution (all items crossed), we print out the moving log.

There is also another use of the moving log: check whether a move has already been done?

```
func hasDoneBefore() -> Bool {
  // check the moving log whether have seen current item positions before?
}
```

Backtracking

The is the core part of the program: the recursive method. Its purpose: make a move if satisfies the constraints.

```
func cross() {

  if is_all_crossed_river? {
    printMovingLog()
    return // exit out of recursion
  }

  for each item in all_items {
    // ignore if not satifsying a move, eg. not going with the farmer

    move(item)

    if is_safe? && !has_done_before? {
      addMoveToMovingLog()
      step += 1
      cross();  // try next move, recursive
    } else {
      undoMove(item)
    }

  }
}
```

10.5 Cryptic Math Equation (Backtracking)

Solve this cryptic equation, each letter stands for a unique digit (0-9). There are no leading zeros.

```
        UK
       USA
 +    USSR
    ---------
     AGING
```

Purpose

- Backtracking to solve number puzzles

Analyze

The brute-force approach (we used in Google Labs Aptitude Test) will work for this puzzle, but won't be elegant. We could use backtracking to solve this puzzle.

We have 8 letters here.

```
 U K S A R G I N
```

For each letter, possible values are 0 - 9. Then our backtracking algorithm can be

- Starting with first letter 'U', assign it possible value '0'
- Then next letter 'K', assign another possible value '1' as long as it has not been used before
- Up to the last letter 'N', then we get a combination
- Check the combination, if not match (most likely), go back one step
- Assign next possible value to 'N', check the new combination
- If run out of possible values for 'N', go back one more step
- Try assign next possible value to 'I'

This might sound complex, but it is how our brain works for a similar but much more simpler puzzles (like 2 or 3 letters). Computers don't mind complex calculations and memorizing all the steps as long as there is algorithm-turned-into-instructions to follow on. Here is the pseudocode for the above backtracking algorithm:

Pseudocode

```
function findOut(letter_index) {

  if all letters are assigned {
    check the answer (converting letter to digits to verify the equation)
    print out solution if matches
    return  // a combination of all 8 letters has been tried
  }

  for each digit (0-9) {
    if satisfy the constraints and the digit not used {
      mark the digit has been used
      assign a digit to this letter (by index)
      findOut(next_letter)
      // the above recurive call returns means 8 letters have been checked
      // make the digit available for next try
      mark the digit not used
    }
  }
}
```

As you can imagine, this will generate a huge number of combinations to check against the equation. It is going to be slow.

Based on equation, we can reason out

- A = 1, U = 9

  Because "USSR" plus 3-digit number (and another 2-digit) can only make 1????, i.e., A = 1 and U = 9.
- G = 0

  Based on A = 1 and U = 9, G must be 0 as U(9) carry 1 to AG (10).

We could go further, but I think this is good enough. Let's leave the rest to the computer to figure out.

End cause

The combination satisfy "UK + USA + USSR = AGING"

Constraints

1. A cannot be 0 (no leading zeroes)
2. U cannot be 0
3. A = 1

4. U = 9
5. G = 0
6. The digit must has not been used to assign to a letter

Hints

Data structure

```
let letters = ["U", "K", "S", "A", "R", "G", "I", "N"]
var isDigitUsed = [0: false, 1: false, 2: false, 3: false, 4: false, 5: false,
                   6: false, 7: false, 8: false, 9: false ]
var letterToDigits = [String: Int]() // Dictionary store the solution
```

letters is defined as array, so that we can start trying first letter letters[0], then letters[1], ..., etc.

isDigitUsed is used to ensure that a digit can only be assigned to one letter.

letterToDigits stores possible combinations, e.g. letterToDigits["U"] => 9; letterToDigits["A"] => 1;

Decode letters to digits

```
func decodeLettersToNumber(letters: String, lookup: [String: Int]) -> Int {
  // construct a number by looking up the hash
  //
  // for example,
  //   decode_letters_to_number("US", {"U" => 1, "S" => 3, "A" => 2})
  // shall return an integer
  //   13
}
```

Check answer

This is to verify whether a possible combination satisfies the equation.

```
func checkAnswer() {
  var uk = decodeLettersToNumber(letters: "UK", lookup: letterToDigits)
  // ...
  // print out the solution if uk + usa + ussr == aging
}
```

10.6 More Puzzle Exercises

Here are some more fun puzzles that are great for programming exercises.

Tower of Hanoi

The object of the game is to move all the disks onto a different pole.

1. Only one disk can be moved at a time.
2. Each move consists of taking the upper disk from one of the stacks and placing it on top of another stack i.e. a disk can only be moved if it is the uppermost disk on a stack.
3. No disk can be placed on top of a smaller disk.

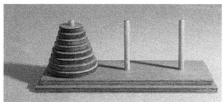
(source: wikipedia[2])

Knight's tour

A knight's tour is a sequence of moves of a knight on a chessboard such that the knight visits every square exactly once.

(source: wikipedia[3])

---

[2]http://en.wikipedia.org/wiki/Tower_of_Hanoi
[3]http://en.wikipedia.org/wiki/Knight%27s_tour

Eight Queens puzzle

Place eight chess queens on an 8x8 chessboard so that no queens is attacking any of the others, that is, no two queens share the same row, column and diagonal.

 (source: wikipedia[4])

---

[4]http://en.wikipedia.org/wiki/Eight_queens_puzzle

11. Mac OS X App - iSpeak

In this chapter, we will build one Cocoa application that run on Mac OS X, using Swift. Obviously, developing a cool app requires a lot knowledge beyond this book. Here I want to give a feel of creating an app with Swift.

iSpeak is a simple text to speech application. A user types in some text and the computer speaks them out.

Of course, we are not going to write a program on how to convert text to speech. It is built-in with the OS X operating system. Try typing the command below in a terminal window.

```
$ /usr/bin/say "Nice to meet you"
```

What we are going to do is write a UI interface to it.

11.1 Create Xcode Cocoa Project

1. On selecting project template, choose "Cocoa Application" under "OS X - Application".

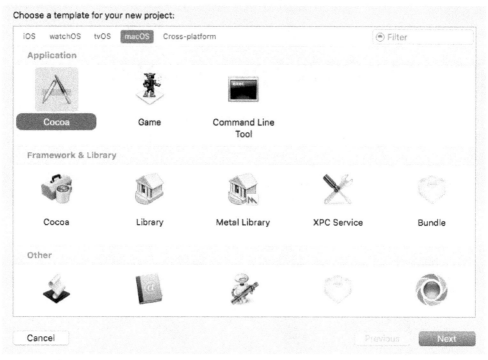

2. Type product name

Choose options for your new project:

Product Name: ex11-iSpeak

Team: None

Organization Name: AgileWay

Organization Identifi... agilway

Bundle Identifier: agilway.ex11-iSpeak

Language: Swift

☐ Use Storyboards
☐ Create Document-Based Application

Document Extension: mydoc

☐ Use Core Data
☐ Include Unit Tests
☐ Include UI Tests

Cancel   Previous   Next

3. Set the project destination

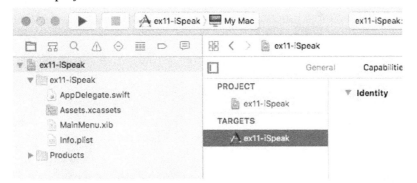

11.2 Design UI in XIB

XIB stands for the XML Interface Builder, which is a used for defining the User Interface (UI) in Xcode.

1. Open Window designer in XIB

Click the 'MainMenu.xib', then the window.

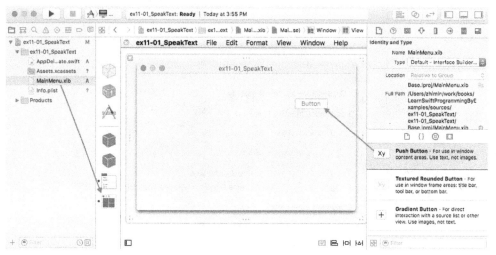

2. Drag controls to the window designer

You may run the application now to see the UI.

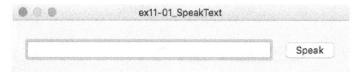

Good, so far. Clicking the 'Speak' button won't do anything yet, as we haven't written one line of code.

11.3 Connect button action

We need to connect the two controls (text field and speak button) in XIB to the code, to make them useful.

1. Show Assistant Editor and XIB

   Open XIB first. Click "Show the Assistant Editor" on the toolbar as shown below.

   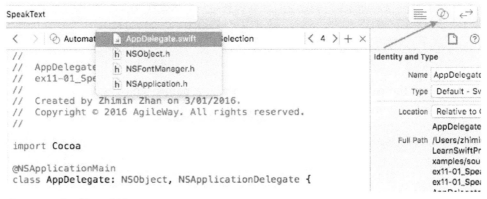

2. Connect the 'Speak' button to `AppDelegate`

   Right click the 'Speak' button and hold, drag to to black place under `func ...`

   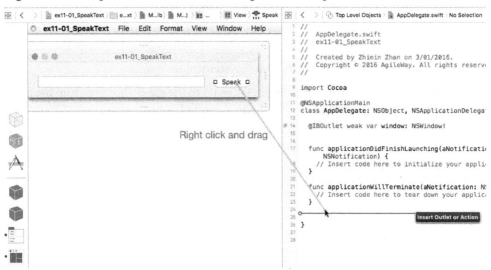

   A connection windows pops out.

3. Change the connection to 'Action', type in a name, which will be the name of the method responding to clicking the button.

4. Click 'Connect' to insert the connection code in `AppDelegate`

```
25    @IBAction func speak(sender: NSButton) {
26    }
27
```

5. Run the application and verify that the connection works.

Add the code `print("Speak button clicked")` in the `speak` function. Run the application and click the 'Speak' button. We the text printed out in console.

```
25    @IBAction func speak(sender: NSButton) {
26        print("Speak button clicked")
27    }
28
29 }
30
```

```
Speak button clicked
Speak button clicked
```

11.4 Connect text field outlet

Now we connect the text field for users to enter text.

1. Connect the text field control to `AppDelegate`

Right click the text field and hold, drag to to black place under `@IBOutlet`.

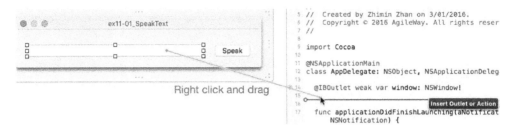

Right click and drag

A connection windows pops out.

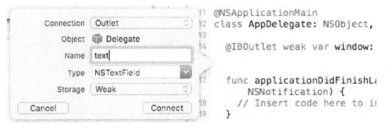

This time, we leave it as Outlet.

2. Type the name of the new outlet and click Connect, Interface Builder adds the declaration for the outlet.

```
14    @IBOutlet weak var window: NSWindow!
15
16    @IBOutlet weak var text: NSTextField!
17
```

11.5 Add code to speak the text

Now the UI works, the missing piece is to invoke the Mac's text to speech utility (/usr/bin/say). In Cocoa, NSTask is used to run another program as a subprocess.

Open `AppDelegate.swift`, change the content of `func speak` to below.

```
@IBAction func speak(_ sender: NSButton) {
  NSLog("Speak button clicked")

  let task: NSTask  = NSTask()
  task.launchPath = "/usr/bin/say"
  task.arguments = ["-v", "fred", text.stringValue]
  task.launch()

  // the statement below will prevent do anything until the tasks finishes
  task.waitUntilExit()
}
```

The logic is quite simple here, just invoke /usr/bin/say with the text 'read' from the text box, in a NSTask.

11.6 Run the app

Run the application from Xcode.

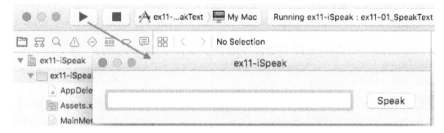

11.7 Distribute the app

The process of packaging the application in a format that it can be installed and run independently (without Xcode) is called App Distribution. There are many settings you can configure and set for an App in Xcode, as this is not the main focus of the book, I will just show the quickest way to get your App out.

In Xcode, select menu 'Product' → 'Scheme' → 'Edit Scheme …'.

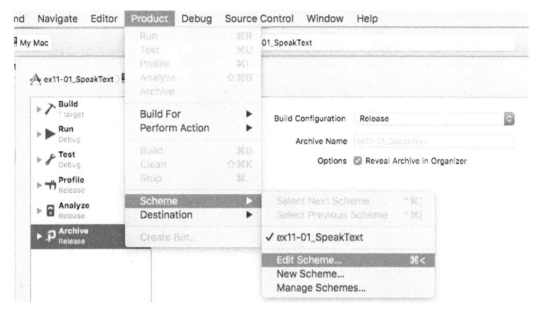

Select "Archive" in the left pane, and choose "Release" for Build Configuration. Generally, for other compiled programming languages as well, there are two build configurations: Debug and Release. Debug builds contains additional information for debugging, which is great for development. Release builds are optimized for performance and smaller size.

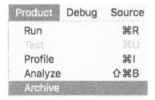

Select menu 'Product' → 'Archive'.

Click "Export ..." button, and you will find the application in a folder on 'Desktop'.

You can compress it in a ZIP archive and share it with your friends.

12. Build iOS App - iCurrency

In this chapter, we will build an iOS app that runs on iPhone, using Swift.

12.1 Design

The purpose of this currency converter app is straightforward: convert local currency to and several foreign currencies. I use US dollar as the local currency as an example, please use your own currency when doing this exercise.

User Interface

Obviously, you can add more and change foreign currencies here. When a user enters an amount in the text box and clicks 'Convert' button, the equivalent amounts in listed currencies are displayed.

To make this app useful, we need to get real (and live) exchange rate. Recall the exercise 8.5, we can use Yahoo finance API. The invoking the URL with embedded two currency codes

```
https://download.finance.yahoo.com/d/quotes.csv?s=USDJPY=X&f=sl1d1t1ba&e=.csv
```

returns

```
"USDJPY=X",112.9600,"3/25/2016","6:54am",112.9600,112.9800
```

`112.9600` is the exchange rate of USD to JPY on 2015-03-25. By using different currency combination, such as `USDEUR` and `AUDJPY`, we can get all the exchange rates of the selected currencies.

Besides UI handling code, the actual code for retrieving exchange rates and conversion is quite simple. You might need to apply the following knowledges learned from previous exercises.

- Looping (convert one to multiple currencies)
- Number calculations
- String to Double
- Display number in a certain format
- Array and Dictionary data structure
- Use of functions
- Use of instance variables

Now, let's turn your design into a reality.

12.2 Create Xcode iOS project

Start up a new Xcode project, select **iOS** → **Application** → **Single View**, and click **Next**.

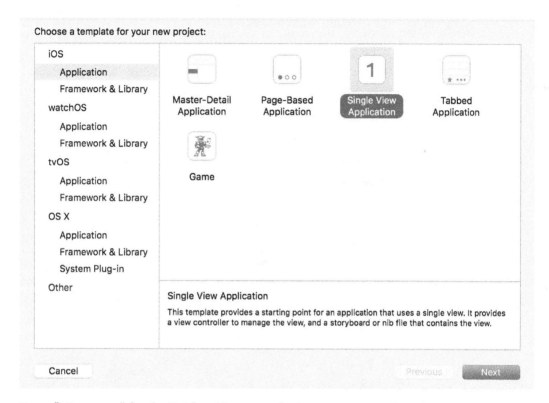

Enter "**iCurrency**" for the Product Name, set the Language to **Swift**, and Devices to **iPhone**. Leave all other checkboxes not checked, and click **Next**.

Choose options for your new project:

Product Name:	iCurrency
Organization Name:	Zhimin Zhan
Organization Identifier:	agileway
Bundle Identifier:	agileway.iCurrency
Language:	Swift
Devices:	iPhone

Use Core Data
Include Unit Tests
Include UI Tests

Cancel   Previous   Next

Choose a directory to save the project, and click **Create**.

Here is what the project looks like.

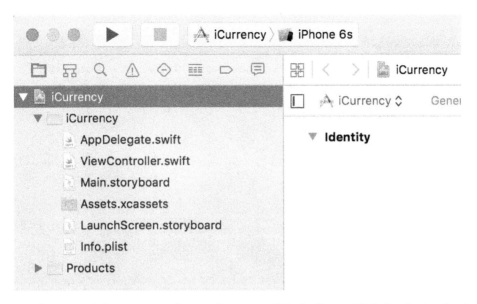

On the upper left, you may choose the target iOS platform. Click the device (such as iPhone 6s) to make a change.

During development, we use iOS Simulators.

Click the Run button, after a short wait, you shall see a blank white screen appear in the Simulator.

Next, we will add UI elements to this screen.

12.3 Xcode Storyboards and Interface Builder

In last chapter, I showed designing UI with XIB. There is an alternative: Storyboards. In fact, Storyboards is the recommended way by Apple for UI design as it is simpler and easier, especially for iOS apps.

Click **Main.storyboard** in the project navigator to reveal the Storyboard in Interface Builder. First, we get the canvas right. Depends on your target platform, click **wAny hAny** at the bottom to select for preferred size. In this case, I select **wCompact hAny**.

Before start dragging UI controls to the storyboard, let's review our design with analyse of control types.

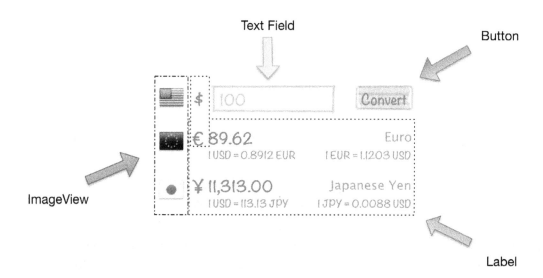

The UI for this app is quite simple, only the following 4 types of UI controls used:

- ImageView
- Button
- Text Field

- Label

Drag the UI controls (from bottom right) to the storyboard based on the design.

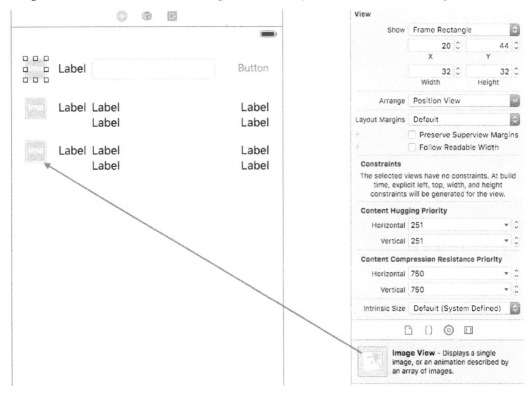

Refine it.

- Change button text to "Convert"
- Set the text field's keyboard type to **Number Pad**

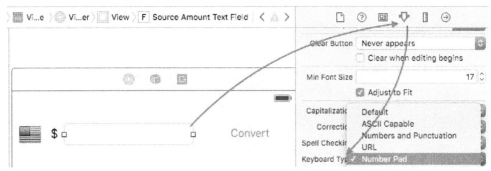

- Change labels of second columns to currency symbols, such as $
- Fill other labels based on your selection of currencies. Don't worry about the accuracy, as these will be replaced by the program.

The storyboard shall look like the below.

You can leave the image views unset for now, I will show how to add images later.

12.4 Link UI to Controller

After we get the basic UI designed, we connect the UI the code. More specifically, **View-Controller**.

When the **Main.storyboard** is open, click "Show the Assistant Editor" on the toolbar. Make sure the **ViewController** is open on the right like below.

Connect button action

Right click **Convert** button in Storyboard to **ViewController** as shown in the above. On the popup windows, select **Action** for *Connection* and enter **convertClicked** for *Name*.

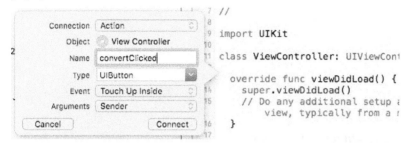

Click **Connect** button, Xcode will insert the following code into **ViewController**.

```
@IBAction func convertClicked(sender: UIButton) {
}
```

This is the function to handle when a user clicks **Convert** button. Let's do a quick test. Just add one print statement in this function.

```
@IBAction func convertClicked(sender: UIButton) {
  print("convert button clicked")
}
```

and then run the application. Click **Convert** button when the app runs in the iOS simulator. You shall see the text "convert button clicked" in the output window.

```
convert button clicked
convert button clicked
convert button clicked



All Output ○                                          🗑  □□
```

This means the connection between the UI and the controller set up successfully.

Connect Text Field and Labels

Continue to connect other UI elements to **ViewController**, except this time, choose **Outlet** for *Connection*.

1. **Text Field** - the amount user entered

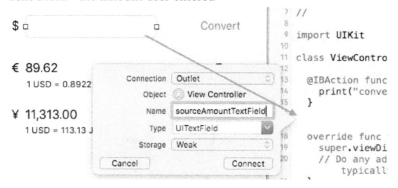

Click **Connect**, Xcode will insert the following statement.

```
@IBOutlet weak var sourceAmount: UITextField!
```

2. **Labels** - the converted amount and rate information

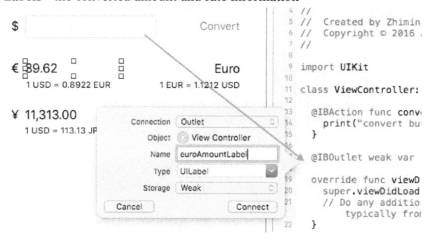

Besides the convert amount labels, we also need to connect the rate and reverse rate labels.

Here is a complete set of referencing actions and outlets in **ViewController**:

```
@IBAction func convertTapped(_ sender: AnyObject) {
  print("convert button clicked")
}

@IBOutlet weak var sourceAmountTextField: UITextField!
@IBOutlet weak var euroAmountLabel: UILabel!
@IBOutlet weak var jpyAmountLabel: UILabel!
@IBOutlet weak var euroRateLabel: UILabel!
@IBOutlet weak var euroReverseRateLabel: UILabel!
@IBOutlet weak var jpyRateLabel: UILabel!
@IBOutlet weak var jpyReverseRateLabel: UILabel!
```

12.5 Add Code Logic

With the UI in place, we add the code into convertClicked function to do:

- Read user entered amount from UI
- Retrieve exchange rates
- Convert currencies
- Display converted amounts in UI

Read user entered amount from UI

Simple, read the text from the text field and convert it (String) to a number.

```
// sourceAmountTextField is a referencing outlet to a text field in Storyboard
let amount = (sourceAmountTextField.text! as NSString).doubleValue
```

Retrieve Exchange Rate

We need to retrieve exchange rates for multiple pairs of currencies, it makes sense to put the code for a live exchange rate between two currencies into a function.

```
// usage: fetchExchangeRate("USD", "JPY")
func fetchExchangeRate(fromCurrency: String, toCurrency:String) -> Double {
  return fetchExchangeRateCurrentyConverterJSON(fromCurrency: fromCurrency, toCurrency:to\
Currency);
}


// deprecated, as Yahoo Finance API is down (or changed)
func fetchExchangeRateYahooFinanceCSV(fromCurrency: String, toCurrency:String) -> Double {
  let urlStr = "https://download.finance.yahoo.com/d/quotes.csv?" +
               "s=\(fromCurrency)\(toCurrency)=X&f=sl1d1t1ba&e=.csv"
  let rateCsvData = getURLContent(url: urlStr)
  let csvParagraphs = rateCsvData.components(separatedBy: ",")
  let exchangeRate = Double(csvParagraphs[1] as String)
  return exchangeRate!;
}


func fetchExchangeRateCurrentyConverterJSON(fromCurrency: String, toCurrency:String) -> D\
ouble {
  let rateJSONData = getURLContent(url: "https://free.currencyconverterapi.com/api/v5/con\
vert?q=" + fromCurrency + "_" + toCurrency + "&compact=y")
  let decoder = JSONDecoder()
  let decodedJson: [String: [String: Double]] = try! decoder.decode([String: [String: Dou\
ble]].self, from: rateJSONData.data(using: .utf8)!)
  return decodedJson[fromCurrency + "_" + toCurrency]!["val"]!
}


func getURLContent(url: String) -> String {
  let urlContent : String = try! String(contentsOf: URL(string: url)!, encoding: String.E\
ncoding.utf8)
  return urlContent
}
```

12.6 Convert currencies

Simple math calculation.

```
var usdEurRate = fetchExchangeRate(fromCurrency: "USD", toCurrency: "EUR")
let euro = amount * usdEurRate
```

Display converted amount in currency format

```
// euroAmountLabel is a referencing outlet to a label in Storyboard
euroAmountLabel.text = formatAmount(number: euro)
```

The function below formats a number to a currency format. For example, `formatAmount(number: 1234.56) -> 1,234.56`.

```
func formatAmount(number:NSNumber) -> String{
  let formatter = NumberFormatter()
  formatter.numberStyle = .currency
  formatter.currencySymbol = ""            // not currency symbol, e.g. $
  formatter.currencyGroupingSeparator = ","
  return formatter.string(from: number)!
}
```

Complete code on conversion

```
@IBAction func convertTapped(_ sender: AnyObject) {
  let amount = (sourceAmountTextField.text! as NSString).doubleValue
  var usdEurRate = fetchExchangeRate(fromCurrency: "USD", toCurrency: "EUR")
  var usdJpyRate = fetchExchangeRate(fromCurrency: "USD", toCurrency: "JPY")

  print("Convert US$\(amount), euro rate: \(usdEurRate), jpy rate: \(usdJpyRate)" )

  let euro = amount * usdEurRate
  let jpy =  amount * usdJpyRate

  euroAmountLabel.text = formatAmount(number: euro)
  jpyAmountLabel.text  = formatAmount(number: jpy)
}
```

12.7 Add Image Assets

Our UI design is not complete, the Image View controls (for the flag of the countries that use that currency) is not set. Firstly, you need to prepare the flag images. In this example, I will use the ones from 365Icon[1] at 32x32 size.

Right click **iCurrency** in the project panel, select **Show in Finder** and create a directory **Images.xcassets** under it.

---

[1]http://365icon.com/icon-styles/ethnic/classic2

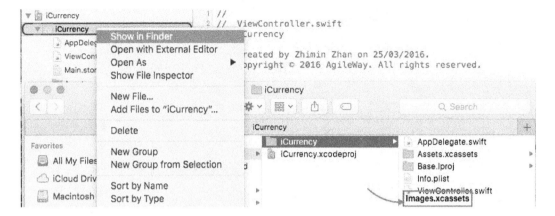

Right click **iCurrency** folder, select **Add Files to 'iCurrency** and choose the newly created **Images.xcassets** directory.

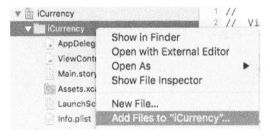

Select **Images.xcassets** in the project panel, click **Import From Project**..., and select the national flag image files prepared earlier.

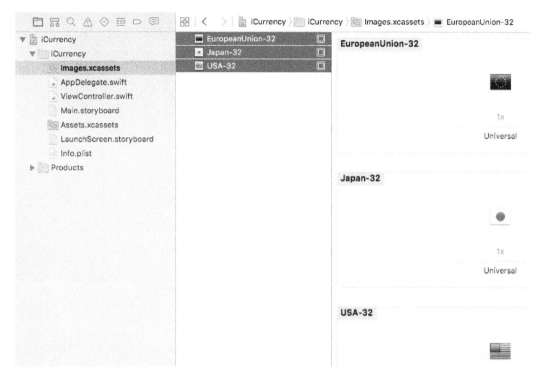

Open **Main.storyboard**, select an Image View control and assign a recently imported image to it. Repeat for the remaining two Image View controls.

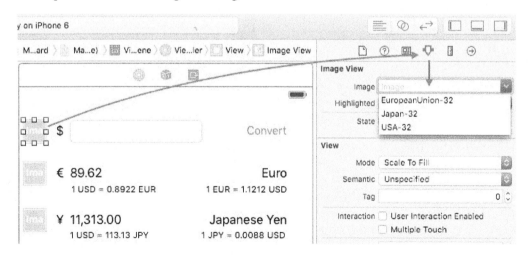

Here is how Storyboard looks after setting images for all three Image Views.

12.8 Add app icon

If an app does not have app icon, it is shown like this on the iOS screen.

Design your icon in two sizes: 120x120 and 180x180 pixels, and export them as PNG images.

Right click **Assets.xcassets** in project panel, select "App Icons & Launch Images" → "New iOS App Icon",

Drag your 120x120 icon to **2x** and 180x180 icon to **3x** for iPhone App iOS 7-9.

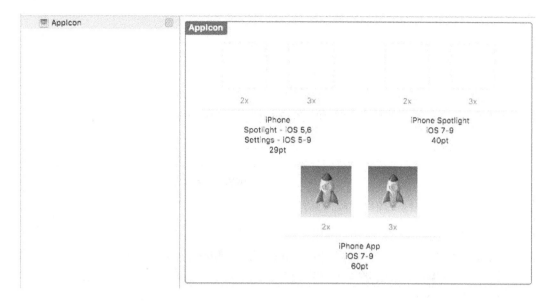

Run your application and you will see the app icon on iOS simulator.

12.9 Optimize

There is a lot room for improvement for this app. I will leave this to you, good news is that most of required knowledge you have learned from the exercises in this book.

- **Display exchange rates**

  On every conversion, we shall update the exchange rates information as well.

  We already have exchange rate and reverse exchange rate for the conversion, to display the rate info is simply constructing a string in a certain format.

- **Cache Exchange Rate**

  Up to now, the program retrieves exchange rates every time a user clicks **Convert** button. Obviously, it is slow and not efficient. Within a short period of time, the same exchange rates shall be used for multiple conversions.

  One approach is to store the exchange rates as an instance variable,

```
// define at class level
var cachedExchangeRateDict = [String: Double]()

// in function does the conversion

  //...
  var rate : Double? = cachedExchangeRateDict["\(sourceCurrency)\(key)"]
  if (rate == nil) {
    // fetch from services
    rate = fetchExchangeRate(fromCurrency: sourceCurrency, toCurrency: key)
    cachedExchangeRateDict["\(sourceCurrency)\(key)"] = rate
  }
  // ...
```

- **Refresh exchange rates manually**

  Related the above, once you implemented the caching (of exchange rates), there shall be a mechanism, typically a refresh button, to allow the user to refresh to get the latest exchange rates.

- **Support new currencies**

  With current design, the foreign currencies are fixed to Euro and JPY. Even at the UI design, I named controls "euroAmountLabel" and hard-coded currency name such as "Japanese Yen" in labels, this is not optimal. If later we want to support adding or removing currencies, this design does not work well.

  A better approach is to separate the data (also called model) from the view. The code below shows all the referencing outlets are named as firstXXX and secondXXX.

```
var allCurrencies = ["USD": "US Dollar", "EUR": "Euro", "CNY": "Chinese Yuan",
                     "JPY": "Japanese Yen", "AUD": "Australian Dollar"]
var currencyAmountUIDict =   [String: UILabel!]()
var currencyRateUIDict =   [String: UILabel!]()
var currencyReverseRateUIDict =   [String: UILabel!]()


// ...
currencyAmountUIDict["EUR"] = firstAmountLabel
currencyAmountUIDict["JPY"] = secondAmountLabel
currencyRateUIDict["EUR"] =    firstRateLabel
currencyReverseRateUIDict["EUR"] = secondReverseRateLabel
```

  The currency name, e.g. Japanese Yen, the converted amount label, e.g. secondAmountLabel, the exchange rate label and the reverse exchange rate label of a currency all can be referenced by a Dictionary using the same key: currency code, e.g. JPY.

12.10 Distribute to your iPhone

Now it is the exciting time, uploading your app to your iPhone. Xcode makes it very simple to do so.

1. Connect the phone to the computer
2. In Xcode, select target device to your phone

3. Run the application

   If it is the first time launching your own apps on iOS devices, you will get the "Untrusted Developer" warning.

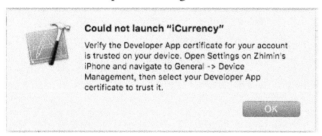

   Here is how to entrust it.

   1. Navigate to **General** → **Device Management** →

   2. Select the certificate (most likely named as your Apple ID), click **Trust** "...@...".
   Relaunch the app.

Appendix 1 Swift in Nutshell

A quick summary of core Swift syntax in code examples.

Print out

```
// print out text
print("a" + "b");    // => "ab"
print(1 + 2)         // => 3
print("1" + "2")     // => "12"

// print out without new line after
print("Hi", terminator: "")
print("Bob")
// the screen output will be "HiBob"
```

Variable assignment

```
var total = 1 + 2 + 3;    // => total has value: 6
var average = total / 3;
print(average)            // => 2

// print string with variable
print("average is \(average)")  // => average is 2
```

Read user input

```
var input1 = readLine()!   // => type 'Hi"
print(input1)              // => "Hi"

// read an integer
print("Enter a number")
var num = Int(readLine()!)
```

Conditional

Two boolean values: true and false

if, else if and else

```
if true {
  print("OK")
} else {
  print("Never reach here")
}

var a = 10
var b = 20
if (a > b) {
  print("a is bigger")
} else if a < b {
  print("b is bigger")
} else {
  print("a,b the same")
}
```

Switch and Case

```
var score = 70
var result = ""

switch score {
 case 0...60 :
   result = "Fail"
 case 60...70 :
   result = "Pass"
 case 71...95 :
   result = "Pass with Distinction"
 case 96, 97, 98, 99:
   result = "Distinction"
 case 100:
   result = "High Distinction"
 default:
   result = "Invalid Score"
}
print(result)
```

Looping

While loop

```
var count = 0
while count < 10 {
  count = count + 1
  print(count)
}
```

For loop

```
for i in 1...3 {
  print(i)
}
// Output: 1 2 3 in three lines
```

Skip loop

```
for i in 1...10 {
  if i % 2 == 0 {
    continue
  }
  print(i)
}
// Output: 1 3 5 7 in four lines
```

Exit Infinite loop

```
var count1 = 0
while true {
  count1 += 1
  print(count1)
  if (count1 > 5) {   // stop at 6
    break
  }
}
// Output: 1 2 3 4 5 6 in six lines
```

Array

```
var scores = [20, 10, 30, 50]
scores.count // => 4
scores.sort()
print(scores) // [10, 20, 30, 50]
scores = [20, 10, 30, 50]
scores.sort { $1 < $0 }
print(scores) //[50, 30, 20, 10]

// return an new array
scores = [20, 10, 30, 50]
let ascScores = scores.sorted{ $0 < $1 }
print(ascScores)    // => new array: [10, 20, 30, 50]
print(scores)       // => unchanged: [20, 10, 30, 50]
```

Accessing array element

```
var mostSpokenLangs = ["Chinese", "Spanish", "English", "Hindi", "Arabic"]
mostSpokenLangs[0] // => "Chinese", indexing starts 0
mostSpokenLangs[2] // => "English"
// mostSpokenLangs[-1]    // => fatal error: Array index out of range

if mostSpokenLangs.contains("Spanish")  {
  print("Yes")
}
```

Add and remove array elements

```
var studentScores = [20, 10, 30, 50]
studentScores.append(80)        // scores: [20,10,30,50, 80]
studentScores.removeAtIndex(2) // scores:  20,10,50, 80]
print(studentScores)            // => [20, 10, 50, 80]
```

Iterate an array

```
for elem in [20, 10, 30] {
  print("Square of \(elem) is \(elem * elem)")
}
```

Output:

```
Square of 20 is 400
Square of 10 is 100
Square of 30 is 900
```

Dictionary

Initialize, add and delete Dictionary elements

```
var usStates = ["CA": "California", "NY": "New York", "TX": "Texas"]
usStates["CA"]    // =>  "California"
usStates.count    // => 3


usStates["FL"] = "Florida"
usStates.count    // => 4


usStates.removeValueForKey("NY")
print(usStates)   // => ["TX": "Texas", "CA": "California", "FL": "Florida"]
```

Iterate a Dictionary

```
var numberLookups = ["one": 1, "two": 2, "three": 3]
for key in numberLookups.keys {
  print("Arabic numeral of \(key) is \(numberLookups[key]!)")
}
```

Output:

```
Arabic numeral of one is 1
Arabic numeral of three is 3
Arabic numeral of two is 2
```

Function

```
func square(num: Int) -> Int {
  return num * num
}
square(num: 6)      // => 36
```

Function that omits the first parameter label

```swift
func square(_ num: Int) -> Int {
  return num * num    // => equal to return num * num
}

print(square(2))    // => 4
print(square(9))    // => 81
```

Function with External Parameter Name

```swift
func square3(number num: Int) -> Int {
  return num * num
}

square3(number: 3)  // => 9
square3(3)          // Error: missing argument label 'number:'
square3(num: 3)  // incorrect argument label in call (have 'num:', expected 'number:')

{:lang="text"}
```

func area(length length: Int, length width: Int) -> Int { return length * width } ~~~

Method arguments with default values

```swift
func exponent(num: Double, power:Double = 2) -> Double {
  return pow(num, power)  // exponential calculation
}

exponent(num: 5)            // => 25
exponent(num: 5, power: 3)  // => 125
```

Scope

```
var d = 1           // variable in scope of file

func add(a: Int, b: Int) -> Int {
  var c = a + b    // local scope of function
  print("inside c = \(c)")
  d = c
  return c
}

var c = 100;       // local scope of outside, different from the c in add()
add(1, b: 2)
print("outside c = \(c)")
print("instance variable d = \(d)")
```

Output:

```
inside c = 3
outside c = 100
instance variable d = 3
```

Nested Loop

```
// times table
for i in 1...9 {
  for j in 1...9 {
    print("\(i) x \(j)  = \(i*j)")
  }
}
```

Class

```swift
class Bird {
  init() { }
  func fly() {
    print("I am flying")
  }
}

class Seagull : Bird {
}

class Parrot : Bird {
  func speak() {
    print("if someone teaches me")
  }
}

var seagull = Seagull()
seagull.fly()   // => "I am flying"

var parrot = Parrot()
parrot.fly()    // => "I am flying"
parrot.speak()  // => "if someone teaches me"

class Ostrich : Bird {

  // Override a method defined in parent class
  override func fly() {
      print("I'd rather run")
  }
}

var ostrich = Ostrich()
ostrich.fly()     // => "I'd rather run"

seagull.speak()  // NoMethodError: undefined method `speak' for #<Seagull:xxx>
```

Protocol Extensions

```
protocol Loggable {
  func log(message: String)
}

extension Loggable {
  func log(message: String) {
    print( "[\(NSDate())] [\(type(of: self))] \(message)");
  }
}

class A
  include Logging
end

class B
  include Logging
end

class C
end

var objA = A()
var objB = B()
var objC = C()

objA.log("in A") // => [2014-11-08 16:07:32 +1000] [A] in A
objB.log("in B") // => [2014-11-08 16:07:32 +1000] [B] in B
objC.log("in C") // => error: value of type 'C' has no member 'log'
```

File I/O

Read file

```
let filePath = "/Users/zhimin/score.txt"
do {
  let fileContent = try NSString(contentsOfFile: filePath, encoding: NSUTF8StringEncoding)
  print(fileContent)
  // ...
} catch var error as NSError {
  print("Error: \(error)")
}
```

Write to file

```
var new_file_content = "Laugh is the best medicine"
try! new_file_content.writeToFile("/Users/zhimin/a_test_file.txt", atomically: true, enco\
ding: NSUTF8StringEncoding)
```

Date

```
var startTime: NSDate = NSDate();  // get current time
print(startTime)  // 2016-01-06 10:10:18 +0000
```

Appendix 2 Solutions

Chapter 2

2.1 Print out Triangle

```
for index in 1...5 {
  let stars = String(repeating: "*", count: index);
  print(stars)
}
```

2.2 Print out a half diamond

```
for row in 1...15 {
  var starCount = row
  if (row > 8) {
    starCount = 16 - row
  }
  let stars = String(repeating: "*", count: starCount);
  print(stars)
}
```

2.3 Print out diamond shape

```
for row in 1...7 {
  var starCount = 0
  var spaceCount = 0

  if (row <= 4) {
    starCount  = row * 2 - 1
    spaceCount = 5 - row
  } else {
    starCount  = (8 - row) * 2 - 1
    spaceCount = row - 3
  }
```

```
  let spaceInFront = String(repeating: " ", count: spaceCount);
  let stars = String(repeating: "*", count: starCount)
  print(spaceInFront + stars)
}
```

2.4 Print big diamond, name your size

```
import Foundation

print("Enter the number of rows for the diamond: ", terminator: "")
var height = Int( readLine()!)
var spaceCount = height! / 2 + 1

for row in (1 ..< height! + 1) {
  var starCount = 0

  if (row <= (height! / 2  + 1) ) {
    starCount  = row * 2 - 1
    spaceCount -= 1
  } else {
    starCount  = (height! - row) * 2 + 1
    spaceCount += 1
  }
  let spaceInFront = String(repeating: " ", count: spaceCount);
  let stars = String(repeating: "*", count: starCount);
  print(spaceInFront + stars)
}
```

Chapter 3

3.1 Simple Add Calculator

```
print("I am an Adding Machine and I am good at it")
print("Enter first number: ", terminator: "")
var num1 = Int(readLine()!)
print("Enter second number: ", terminator: "")
var num2 = Int(readLine()!)

print("Thinking...")
var answer = num1! + num2!
print("Got it, the answer is: \(answer)")
```

3.2 Addition Quiz

```
var count = 0
for index in 1...10 {
  var num1 = Int.random(in: 0..<10)
  var num2 = Int.random(in: 0..<10)
  print("\(num1) + \(num2) = ", terminator: "")
  var theAnswer = num1 + num2

  var userAnswer = Int(readLine()!)

  if theAnswer == userAnswer {
    print("Correct!")
    count += 1
  } else {
    print("Wrong!")
  }
}
print("Your score is \(count)/10")
```

Courtney forgot the "You score: " part, which she added later.

3.3 Subtraction Quiz

```swift
var count = 0
for _ in 1...10 {
  var num1 = Int.random(in: 0..<10)
  var num2 = Int.random(in: 0..<10)
  var theAnswer = 0

  if num1 > num2 {
    print("\(num1) - \(num2) = ", terminator: "")
    theAnswer = num1 - num2
  } else {
    print("\(num2) - \(num1) = ", terminator: "")
    theAnswer = num2 - num1
  }

  var userAnswer = Int(readLine()!)
  if theAnswer == userAnswer {
    print("Correct!")
    count += 1
  } else {
    print("Wrong!")
  }
}

print("Your score is \(count)/10")
```

3.4 Number Guessing Game

```swift
print("I have a secret number (0-9) Can you guess it?")
var count = 0
var secretNumber = Int.random(in: 0..<10)

while var input = Int(readLine()!) {
  count += 1
  if input > secretNumber {
    print("TOO BIG")
  } else if input < secretNumber {
    print("too small")
  } else {
    print("CORRECT")
    break
  }
}
```

```
print("The number is : \(secretNumber). and you guessed \(count) times!!")
```

Chapter 4

4.1 Sort Children Names

```
var kidNames: [String] = []
var userInput: String;

print("Enter child names in class: (0 to finish)")

repeat {
  userInput = readLine()!
  if userInput != "0" {
    kidNames.insert(userInput, at: 0)
  } else {

  }
} while userInput != "0"

print("Kids in order :")
kidNames.sort { $0 < $1 }
print(kidNames)
```

4.2 Get the character from given alphabetical position

```
var array: [String] = ["A", "B", "C", "D", "E", "F", "G", "H", "I", "J", "K", "L", "M", "\
N", "O", "P", "Q", "R", "S", "T", "U", "V", "W", "X", "Y", "Z"]

print("I know the alpha bet very well, enter the alphabetical order number (integer) and \
I will tell you the corresponding letter, 0 to quit:")

while true {
  var userInput = Int(readLine()!)
  if userInput == 0 {
    break
  }
  var n = userInput! - 1
  print(array[n])
}
```

4.3 Calculate Average

```
var array: [Int] = []
var count = 0
print("Enter scores: ")

while true {
        let input = Int(readLine()!)
  if input == -1 {
    break
  }
        array.insert(input!, at: 0)
        count += 1
}

var theSum = array.reduce(0, +)
var average = theSum / count
print("Average score: \(average)")
```

4.4 What makes 100% in life?

If we represent the alphabet numerically by identifying sequence of letters (A,B,C,...,X,Y,Z) with the percentages (1%,2%,3%,...,24%,25%,26%). A sum of each characters' value in a word is the meaning to life percentage. Then

H-A-R-D-W-O-R-K = $(8+1+18+4+23+15+18+11)\% = 98\%$

Ask user to enter an English word (or string) and calculate its meaning to life percentage.

```
Enter your word (in capital): HARDWORK
The value of meaning to life: 98%
```

Solution

```
var alphaValues = [String: Int]()

let alphabets = ["A","B","C","D","E","F","G","H","I","J","K","L","M","N","O","P","Q","R",\
"S","T","U","V","W","X","Y","Z"]

for (index, value) in alphabets.enumerated() {
  alphaValues[value] = index + 1
}

print("Enter word in capitals: ")
var input = readLine()!

var theValue = 0
for character in input {
    theValue = theValue + (alphaValues[String(character)])!
}

print("The value of meaning to life: \(theValue)%")
```

Chapter 5

5.1 Fahrenheit to Celsius Converter

```
print("Enter temperature in Fahrenheit: ", terminator: "")
var input = (readLine()! as NSString).floatValue
var celsius = (input - 32) * 5.0 / 9.0
print("In Celsius: ", terminator: "")
print(round(celsius * 10) / 10)
```

5.2 Personal Income Tax Calculator

```
print("Enter your annual income: ", terminator: "")
var income = (readLine()! as NSString).floatValue
var tax : Float = 0.0

switch (income) {
case 0...18200:
  print ("No Tax")
case 18201...37000:
  tax = (income - 18200) * 0.19
case 37001...80000:
  tax = (income - 37000) * 0.325 + 3572
case 80001...180000:
  tax = (income - 80000) * 0.37 + 17547
default:
  tax = (income - 180000) * 0.45 + 54547
}

print("Your personal income tax amount: $\(tax)")
```

5.3 Word count

```
var text = "Everybody in this country should learn how to program a computer...  because \
it teaches you how to think.\n - Steve Jobs"
var words = text.components(separatedBy: CharacterSet.whitespaces)
var word_count = words.count
print("The text has \(word_count) words")
```

5.4 Generate Lotto Numbers

```
var count = 0
var lotteryNumbers: [Int] = [];

while count <  6 {
  var lotto_number = Int(arc4random_uniform(49)) + 1
  if lotteryNumbers.contains(lotto_number) {
    // print("ALREADY HAS #{lotto_number}")
    continue
  } else {
    lotteryNumbers.append(lotto_number)
    count += 1
  }
}
```

```
print("Your winning lottery numbers are \(lotteryNumbers), good luck!")
```

5.5 Number sorting

```
var array = [2, 8, 7, 3, 4, 5, 9, 1, 10, 6]

for idx in 0...array.count-2 {
  // print(idx)
  for idx2 in (idx+1)...(array.count-1)  {
    if array[idx] > array[idx2] {
      let temporaryA = array[idx]
      array[idx] = array[idx2]
      array[idx2] = temporaryA
    }
  }
}
print("The numbers in order: \(array)")
```

Chapter 6

6.1 Finding Divisors

```
var divisors: [Int] = []
print("Enter a number: ", terminator: "")
var input = Int(readLine()!)!

for x in 1...input {
        var check = input % x
        if check == 0 {
          divisors.append(x)
        }
}
print("The divisors of \(input): \(divisors)")
```

6.2 Finding the Highest Common Factor

```
var divisorsList1: [Int] = []
var divisorsList2: [Int] = []

print("Enter first number: ", terminator: "")
var num1 = Int(readLine()!)
for x in 1...num1! {
  var check = num1! % x
  if check == 0 {
    divisorsList1.append(x)
  }
}

print("Enter second number: ", terminator: "")
var num2 = Int(readLine()!)
for x in 1...num2! {
    var check = num2! % x
    if check == 0 {
        divisorsList2.append(x)
    }
}

divisorsList1.sort { $1 < $0 }

for value in divisorsList1 {
  if divisorsList2.contains(value) {
    print("The HCF is \(value)")
    break
  }
}
```

6.3 Finding the Least Common Multiple (LCM)

```
print("Enter the first number: ", terminator: "")
var num1 = Int(readLine()!)

print("Enter the second number:", terminator: "")
var num2 = Int(readLine()!)

var check = 0;
if num1! > num2! {
  check = num1!
} else {
  check = num2!
}

var startTime: Date = Date();
for n in (check ..< num1! * num2! + 1) where n % check == 0 {
  if n % num1! == 0 && n % num2! == 0 {
    print("The LCM for \(num1!) and \(num2!) is \(n)")
    break
  }
}
var finishTime: Date = Date();
var duration = finishTime.timeIntervalSince(startTime)
print("The time took is \(duration) seconds")
```

6.4 Finding Prime Numbers

```
var primeNumbers: [Int] = []
for num in (2...20) {  // check one number is a prime number or not
  var flag = true
  if num == 2 {
    primeNumbers.append(num)
    continue
  }

  for x in (2...num-1) { // trying to check each possible divisor
    if num % x == 0 {
      flag = false // mark this has divisor
      break // no point to check more - composite, moves on to next
    }
  }

  if flag {  // the number has no divisors
    primeNumbers.append(num) // add to prime number list
```

```
  }
}

print("Prime numbers (up to 20) are : \(primeNumbers)")
```

6.5 Fibonacci sequence

```
var hibNumbers: [Int] = [1, 1]
var num1 = 1
var num2 = 1

for _ in 1...10  {
  var nextNumber = num1 + num2
  hibNumbers.append(nextNumber)
  num1 = num2
  num2 = nextNumber
}
print("The number of rabbit pairs are: \(hibNumbers)")
```

6.6 Consecutive Sums

```
extension Array {
  func combine(separator: String) -> String{
    var str : String = ""
    for (idx, item) in self.enumerated() {
      str += "\(item)"
      if idx < self.count-1 {
        str += separator
      }
    }
    return str
  }
}

print("Enter a number: ", terminator: "")

var x = Int(readLine()!)
var y = (x! + 1) / 2

for startingNumber in 1...y-1  {
  // println("starting num = \(startingNumber)")
  for j in startingNumber...y {
```

```
      var sum = Array(startingNumber...j).reduce(0, +)
      if sum == x {
        print("\(x!) = ", terminator: "")
        var elements = Array(startingNumber...j)
        print( elements.combine(separator: " + ") )
      }
    }
  }
}
```

Chapter 7

7.1 Finding the Highest Common Factor (using method)

```
func getDivisors(num: Int) -> [Int]{
  var divisors: [Int] = []

  for x in 1...num {
    let check = num % x
    if check == 0 {
        divisors.append(x)
    }
  }
  return divisors
}

print("Enter first number: ", terminator: "")
var num1 = Int(readLine()!)
var divisors_list_1 = getDivisors(num: num1!)
print("Enter second number: ", terminator: "")
var num2 = Int(readLine()!)
var divisors_list_2 = getDivisors(num: num2!)

divisors_list_1.sort { $1 < $0 }
for value in divisors_list_1 {
  if divisors_list_2.contains(value) {
    print("The HCF is \(value)")
    break
  }
}
```

7.2 Generate Lotto Numbers (using a method)

```
func getNextValidLotteryNumber(existingNumbers: [Int])  -> Int {
  var lottoNumber = Int(arc4random_uniform(49)) + 1
  while existingNumbers.contains(lottoNumber) {
    lottoNumber = Int(arc4random_uniform(49)) + 1
  }
  return lottoNumber
}
var count = 0
var lotteryNumbers: [Int] = [];
while count <  6 {
  lotteryNumbers.append( getNextValidLotteryNumber(existingNumbers: lotteryNumbers) )
  count += 1
}
print("Your winning lottery numbers are \(lotteryNumbers), good luck!")
```

7.3 Finding the LCM for multiple numbers (using method)

```
// return lcm for a and b
func lcm(a: Int, b: Int) -> Int {
  for n in a...a*b  {
    if n % a == 0 && n % b == 0 {
        return n
    } // end of if
  } // end of loop
  return a * b
}

var m = 1
for w in 2...15 {
  m = lcm(a: m, b: w)
}
print("The lowest number that is dividable by 1 to 15 is: \(m)")
```

Chapter 8

8.1 Calculate average score

```
let path:String = "\(NSHomeDirectory())/work/swiftcode/files/score.txt"

var content:String = ""

// error handling, introduced in Swift 2
do {
  content = try String(contentsOfFile: path, encoding: String.Encoding.utf8)
} catch let err as NSError {
  print("Reading file Error: \(err) on reading file: \(path)")
}

var strArray = content.components(separatedBy: "\n")
var intArray: [Int] = []

for str in strArray  {
  if str != "" {
    intArray.append(Int(str)!)
  }
}
var theSum: Int = intArray.reduce(0, +)
// error if only one is Float type
let theAverage = Float(theSum) / Float(intArray.count)
print("Average score is " + String(format: "%0.1f", theAverage) )
```

8.2 Count words and lines in a text file

```
// Usage: swift count_words_lines.swift /Users/zhimin/novel.txt

let firstCommandLineArgument = CommandLine.arguments[0] // the program
let secondCommandLineArgument = CommandLine.arguments[1]

print("First: '\(firstCommandLineArgument)'")
print("Processing file '\(secondCommandLineArgument)'")

let filePath = secondCommandLineArgument
let fileContent = try String(contentsOfFile: filePath, encoding: String.Encoding.utf8)

var wordCount = fileContent.components(separatedBy: CharacterSet.whitespaces).count
var lineCount = fileContent.components(separatedBy: "\n").count
print("\(secondCommandLineArgument) contains \(wordCount) words in \(lineCount) lines")
```

8.3 Mail merge birthday invitation cards

```
let guestList = ["Pokkle", "Angela", "Tonpa", "Toby", "Biscuit", "Mito", "Kate", "Renee",\
 "Chloe", "Kelly", "Melody"]

let invitation: String = "Dear {{first_name}}, \n\nI am celebrating my 12th Birthday on t\
he 1st of April!\nCome celebrate with me! \n\nWhere: 42 Greed-Island Street, Yorkshin Cit\
y\nWhen: 2PM to 5PM\nRSVP: 24th of March (0400-000-000 or rsvpjessica@gmail.com)\n\nHope \
to see you there,\n\nJessica.\n";

for guest in guestList {
  let named_invitation = invitation.replacingOccurrences(of: "{{first_name}}", with: gues\
t)
  print(named_invitation)
  do {
    try named_invitation.write(toFile: "/Users/zhimin/\(guest.lowercased())_invitations.t\
xt", atomically: false, encoding: String.Encoding.utf8)
  } catch _ {
  }
}
```

8.4 Rename files

```
let folderPath = "\(NSHomeDirectory())/work/swiftcode/files/book_dir"

let fileManager = FileManager.default
let enumerator:FileManager.DirectoryEnumerator = fileManager.enumerator(atPath: folderPat\
h)!

while let fileName = enumerator.nextObject() as? String {

  let re = try! NSRegularExpression(pattern: "chapter\\s(\\d+)(.*)", options: [])

  let matches = re.matches(in: fileName, options: [],
                           range: NSRange(location: 0, length: fileName.utf16.count ))

  if matches.count == 0 {  // no matches
    continue
  }

  let firstMatch = matches[0]

  let originFilePath:String = folderPath + "/" + fileName
  var newFileName:String = ""
```

```
  // range at index 0: full match
  // range at index 1: first capture group

  let chapterNo = (fileName as NSString).substring(with: firstMatch.range(at: 1))
  var newSeq = chapterNo
  if (Int(chapterNo)! < 10) {
    newSeq = "0" + chapterNo
  }

  let fileExt = (fileName as NSString).substring(with: firstMatch.range(at: 2))
  newFileName = "chapter_\(newSeq)\(fileExt)"

  let newFilePath:String = folderPath + "/" + newFileName
  if newFileName.utf16.count > 0 {
    print("Rename \(originFilePath) to \(newFilePath)")
    var moveError: NSError?
    do {
      try fileManager.moveItem(atPath: originFilePath, toPath: newFilePath)
    } catch let error as NSError {
      moveError = error
      print(moveError!.localizedDescription)
    }
  }

}
```

8.5 Currency exchange with life quoting

```
func getURLContent(url: String) -> String {
  let urlColntent : String = try! String(contentsOf: URL(string: url)!, encoding: String.\
Encoding.utf8)
  return urlColntent as String
}

func fetchExchangeRateCSV(fromCurrency: String,  toCurrency: String) -> Double {
  let rateCsvData = getURLContent(url: "http://download.finance.yahoo.com/d/quotes.csv?s=\
" + fromCurrency + toCurrency + "=X&f=sl1d1t1ba&e=.csv")
  let csvParagraphs = rateCsvData.components(separatedBy: ",")
  return Double(csvParagraphs[1] as String)!
}

// get exchange rate in JSON format:
func fetchExchangeRateJSON(fromCurrency: String,  toCurrency: String) -> Double {
```

```
    let rateJSONData = getURLContent(url: "https://free.currencyconverterapi.com/api/v5/c\
onvert?q=" + fromCurrency + "_" + toCurrency + "&compact=y")
    let decoder = JSONDecoder()
    let decodedJson: [String: [String: Double]] = try! decoder.decode([String: [String: D\
ouble]].self, from: rateJSONData.data(using: .utf8)!)
    return decodedJson[fromCurrency + "_" + toCurrency]!["val"]!
}

let exchangeRate = fetchExchangeRateJSON(fromCurrency: "AUD", toCurrency: "JPY")
// print(exchangeRate)

print("Enter the amount of Australian dollars: ", terminator: "")
var audAmountStr:String = readLine()!
var audAmount:Double = Double(audAmountStr)!
var jpyAmount = audAmount * exchangeRate
print("=> ¥" + String(format: "%0.2f", jpyAmount)
```

Chapter 9

9.1 Calculator (Class)

```
class Calculator {
  func add(one: Int, another: Int) -> Int {
    return one + another
  }
  func minus(one: Int, another: Int) -> Int {
    return one - another
  }
}

var calc = Calculator()
print( calc.add(one: 2, another: 3) )
print( calc.minus(one: 17, another: calc.add(one: 2, another:3) ) )
```

9.2 Age of Teacher and Students

```swift
class Person {
  var name : String
  var birthDate: Date
  var gender: String?

  init(name: String, birthDate: String) {
    self.name = name

    let dateFormatter = DateFormatter()
    dateFormatter.dateFormat = "YYYY-MM-DD"
    self.birthDate = dateFormatter.date(from: birthDate)!
  }

  func age() -> Int {
    let calendar  = Calendar.current;
    let ageComponents = (calendar as NSCalendar).components(.year,
        from: self.birthDate,
        to: Date(),
        options: [])

    return ageComponents.year!
  }

}

class Teacher : Person {

}

class Student : Person {
  var grade: Int
  init(name: String , birthDate: String, grade: Int) {
    self.grade = grade
    super.init(name: name, birthDate: birthDate)
  }
}


var teacher_1 = Teacher(name: "James Bond", birthDate: "1968-04-03")
var teacher_2 = Teacher(name: "Michael Zasky", birthDate: "1978-01-02")

print("Teacher '\(teacher_1.name)' age: \(teacher_1.age())")
```

```
var avgTeacherAge =  (teacher_1.age() + teacher_2.age() ) / 2;
print( "Average Teacher age: \(avgTeacherAge)")

var students = [Student]()
students.append(Student(name: "John Sully", birthDate: "1999-10-03", grade: 10))
students.append(Student(name: "Michael Page", birthDate: "1999-05-07", grade:11))
students.append(Student(name: "Anna Boyle", birthDate: "1998-12-03", grade:10))
students.append(Student(name: "Dominic Chan", birthDate: "1999-09-10", grade:10))


var grade10StudentAges = [Int]()
for student in students {
  if student.grade == 10 {
    grade10StudentAges.append(student.age())
  }
}
var avgGrade10StudentAge = grade10StudentAges.reduce(0, +) / grade10StudentAges.count
print("Average Grade 10 students age: \(avgGrade10StudentAge)")
```

9.3 Calculate Sales Tax

```
let GST_RATE = 10.0

// defined an interface
protocol Taxable {

  var amount: Double { get set }
  var sales_tax_applicable: Bool { get set }

  func net_amount() -> Double
  func gst() -> Double
}

// an implementation of interface
extension Taxable {

  func net_amount() -> Double {
    var the_amount:Double
    if self.sales_tax_applicable {
      the_amount = (self.amount / (100.0 + GST_RATE) * 100.0)
    } else {
      the_amount =  self.amount
    }
```

```
      return round(the_amount * 100) / 100
  }

  func gst() -> Double {
    var tax:Double
    if self.sales_tax_applicable {
      tax = (self.amount - self.net_amount())
    } else {
      tax = 0.0
    }
    tax =  round(tax * 100) / 100
    return tax
  }

}

class ServiceItem : Taxable {
  var name: String
  var amount: Double
  var sales_tax_applicable: Bool

  init(name: String, amount: Double) {
    self.name = name
    self.amount = amount
    self.sales_tax_applicable = false    // => default no sales tax
  }
}

class Goods : Taxable {
  var name: String
  var amount: Double
  var sales_tax_applicable: Bool

  init(name: String, amount: Double) {
    self.name = name
    self.amount = amount
    self.sales_tax_applicable = true    // => default no sales tax
  }
}

var foam_roller = Goods(name: "Foam Roller", amount: 49.95);
print("\(foam_roller.name) Net Amount: \(foam_roller.net_amount()), GST: \(foam_roller.gs\
t())");
```

```
var physio_service = ServiceItem(name: "Physio Consultation", amount: 120.0);
print("\(physio_service.name) Net Amount: \(physio_service.net_amount()), GST: \(physio_s\
ervice.gst())");

var pilates_class = ServiceItem(name: "Pilates Classes", amount: 80.0)
pilates_class.sales_tax_applicable = true
print("\(pilates_class.name) Net Amount: \(pilates_class.net_amount()), GST: \(pilates_cl\
ass.gst())")
```

9.4 Library System

```
class Library {

  static var books:    [Book] = []
  static var members: [Member] = []
  static var rentals: [Rental] = []

  class func importBooks(csvFilePath: String) {
    var fileContent = ""
    do {
      fileContent = try String(contentsOfFile: csvFilePath, encoding: String.Encoding.utf\
8)
    } catch let error as NSError {
      print("Error: \(error)")
    }

    let lines = fileContent.components(separatedBy: "\n")
    for var line in lines {
      var fields = line.components(separatedBy: ",")
      if fields.count < 2 || fields[0] == "TITLE" { // empty file or heading row
        continue
      }
      books.append( Book(title: fields[0], author: fields[1]) )
    }

  }

  class func findByTitle(title: String) -> Book? {
    var the_book: Book?
    for book in self.books {
      if book.title == title {
        the_book = book
```

```
        return the_book
      }
    }
    print("Book '\(title)' not found")
    return the_book
  }

  class func bookCount() -> Int {
    return books.count
  }

  class func borrow(_ member: Member, book: Book) {
    if book.status == "available" {
      rentals.append( Rental(member: member, book: book) )
      book.status = "checked out"
      print("\(member.name) borrows '\(book.title)' OK.")
    } else {
      print("The book '\(book.title)' is not available!")
    }
  }

  class func returnBook(_ book: Book) {
    var the_rental: Rental?

    for rental in rentals {
      if rental.book === book {
        the_rental = rental // found the rental record
        break
      }
    }

    if the_rental != nil {
      the_rental?.finish()
      print("The book '\(the_rental!.book.title)' is returned.")
      book.status = "available"
    }

  }

}

class Book {
```

```
  var title: String
  var author: String
  var status: String = String()

  init(title: String, author: String) {
    self.title = title
    self.author = author
    self.status = "available"
  }

}

class Member {
  var name: String
  var memberId: String

  init(name: String, memberId: String) {
    self.name = name
    self.memberId = memberId
  }
}


class Rental {
  var member: Member
  var book: Book
  var is_active: Bool = false

  init(member: Member, book: Book) {
    self.member = member
    self.book = book
    self.is_active = true
  }

  func finish(){
    self.is_active = false
  }

}

let booksCsvFile  = "\(NSHomeDirectory())/work/swiftcode/files/books.csv"
Library.importBooks(csvFilePath: booksCsvFile)
print(Library.bookCount()) // => 10
```

```
var john = Member(name: "John Sully", memberId: "1001")
var mike = Member(name: "Mike Zasky", memberId: "1002")

var book = Library.findByTitle(title: "Practical Web Test Automation")
print(book)

Library.borrow(john, book: book!)
Library.borrow(mike, book: book!)
Library.returnBook(book!)
Library.borrow(mike, book: book!)
```

9.5 Sunflower vs Zombies Simulation

```
let DISTANCE:Int = 10

class Sunflower {
  var health: Int

  init() {
    health = 100
  }

  func exchangeFire(zombie: Zombie) {

    if zombie.in_touch_distance() {
      health -= 5
    } else {
      health -= ( Int(arc4random() % 2) + 1)
    }

    if health <= 0 {
      health = 0
    }

    zombie.health -= ( Int(arc4random() % 31) + 10) // between 10 to 40 damage

    if zombie.health <= 0 {
      zombie.die()
    } else {
      zombie.move_forward()
    }
```

```
    }

}

class Zombie {

  var health: Int
  var step: Int
  var movingSpeed: Int

  // static variable (not class variable, not inherited by subclass)
  static var liveCount :Int = 0

  init() {
    health = 100
    step = 0
    movingSpeed = (arc4random() % 10) >= 8  ?  2 : 1 //  80% are jumping zombies
    Zombie.liveCount += 1
  }

  func die() {
    health = 0
    Zombie.liveCount -= 1
  }

  func is_dead() -> Bool {
    return health <= 0
  }

  func in_touch_distance() -> Bool {
    return step == DISTANCE
  }

  func move_forward() {
    step += movingSpeed
    if step >= DISTANCE {
      step = DISTANCE
    }
  }

}
```

```
let ZOMBIES_COUNT = 15
print("\nY(100)   ___ ___ ___ ___ ___ ___ ___ ___ ___ ___", terminator: "")

let sunflower = Sunflower()
var zombies = [Zombie]()
for i in 1...ZOMBIES_COUNT {
    zombies.append(Zombie())
}

var active_zombie: Zombie = zombies[0]

while (sunflower.health > 0) {
  // sleep(1000) // adjust game speed, smaller number, faster
  Thread.sleep(forTimeInterval: 0.1)

  if active_zombie.is_dead() {
    if zombies.count > 0 {
      active_zombie = zombies.remove(at: 0)
    }
  }

  if zombies.count == 0 {
    break
  }

  sunflower.exchangeFire(zombie: active_zombie)

  var flower_health_str = String(format: "%2d", sunflower.health)
  print("\r", terminator: "")
  print("F(\(flower_health_str))  ", terminator: "")

  var zombie_health = String(format: "%2d", active_zombie.health)
  var zombie_pos = "Z\(zombie_health)"

  var fields : [String] = []

  for index in 0...9 {
    if active_zombie.step == (10-index) {
      fields.append(zombie_pos)
    } else {
      fields.append("___")
    }
  }
```

```
  print(fields.joined(separator: " "), terminator: "") // print out pos without new line
  fflush(__stdoutp) // flush stdout to see moving effect
}

if sunflower.health > 0 {
  print("\nYou Win! The sunflower survived attacks from \(ZOMBIES_COUNT) zombies.")
} else {
  print("\nGame Over!")
}
```

Chapter 10

10.1 Google Labs Aptitude Test

```
for w in 1...9 {

  for d in 1...9 {
    if (d == w) {
        continue
    }

    for o in 0...9 {
      if (o == d  || o == w) {
          continue
      }

      for t in 0...9 {
        if (t == o || t == d  || t == w) {
            continue
        }

        for g in 0...9 {
          if (g == t || g == o || g == d ||  g == w) {
              continue
          }

          for l in 0...9  {
            if (l == g || l == t || l == o || l == d || l == w), {
                continue
            }
```

```
for e in 0...9 {
  if (e == l || e == g || e == t || e == o || e == d || e == w) {
    continue
  }

  for c in 0...9 {
    if (c==e || c==l || c==g || c==t || c==o || c==d || c==w) {
        continue
    }

    for m in 0...9  {
      if (m==c || m==e || m==l || m==g || m==t || m==o || m==d || m==w) {
        continue
      }

      var top_no =    w*100000 + w*10000 + w*1000 + d*100 + o*10 + t
      var bottom_no = g*100000 + o*10000 + o*1000 + g*100 + l*10 + e
      var result =    d*100000 + o*10000 + t*1000 + c*100 + o*10 + m

      if ( (top_no - bottom_no) == result) {
        print("\(top_no) - \(bottom_no) = \(result)")
      }
    }
  }
}
}



}
}
}
```

10.2 Fibonacci (Recursion)

```swift
func fibonacci(num:Int) -> Int {
  if (num <= 1) {
    return num
  }
  return fibonacci(num: num - 1) + fibonacci(num: num - 2)
}
print( fibonacci(num: 10) )   // => 55
```

10.2 HCF (Recursion)

```swift
func hcf(a: Int, b: Int) -> Int  {
  if (a == 0) {
    return b
  } else if (b == 0) {
    return a
  } else {
    return hcf(a: b, b: a % b)
  }
}


print( hcf(a: 2480, b: 1960) )
```

10.3 Compound Interest

```swift
func compoundInterest(principal: Float, rate: Float, years: Int) -> Float {
  if (years == 0) {
    return principal
  } else {
    return compoundInterest(principal: principal * (1 + rate), rate: rate, years: years-1)
  }
}


print("Enter deposited amount : $", terminator: "")
var amount = Float(readLine()!)!
print("Enter interest rate (8% enter 0.08): ", terminator: "")
var rate = Float( readLine()! )!
print("For how long (years): ", terminator: "")
var years = Int(readLine()!)
print("")


var theTotal = compoundInterest(principal: amount, rate: rate, years: years!)
print( "After \(years!) years, you will get $\(theTotal)" )
```

10.4 Farmer Crosses River Puzzle

```swift
var itemPositions = ["farmer": "not_crossed", "wolf": "not_crossed", "sheep": "not_crosse\
d", "cabbage": "not_crossed" ]
let items = ["farmer", "wolf", "sheep", "cabbage"]
var step = 1
var direction = "forward"  // default, another value "backward"
var movingLog = [ 0: itemPositions ];

func isAllCrossedRiver() -> Bool {
  var allCrossed = true
  for (_, status) in itemPositions {
    if (status == "not_crossed") {
      allCrossed = false
    }
  }
  return allCrossed
}

func printMovingLog() {
  let sortedDict = movingLog.sorted { $0.0 < $1.0 }
  for (step, positions) in sortedDict {

    var actionStr = "Step \(step)"

    var itemsNotCrossed = Set<String>()
    var itemsCrossed = Set<String>()

    for (item, status) in positions {
      if (status == "not_crossed") {
        itemsNotCrossed.insert(item)
      } else {
        itemsCrossed.insert(item)
      }
    }

    if (step > 0) {
      let prevItemPositions = movingLog[step - 1]

      var prev_itemsNotCrossed = [String]()
      var prev_itemsCrossed = [String]()

      for (item, status) in prevItemPositions! {
        if (status == "not_crossed") {
```

```swift
          prev_itemsNotCrossed.append(item)
        } else {
          prev_itemsCrossed.append(item)
        }
      }

      let diffCrosssed = itemsCrossed.subtracting(prev_itemsCrossed)
      let diffNotCrossed = itemsNotCrossed.subtracting(prev_itemsNotCrossed)

      if (diffCrosssed.count > 0) {
        actionStr += " \(diffCrosssed) forward"
      } else {
        actionStr += " \(diffNotCrossed) backward"
      }

    }

    print(actionStr);
    print("        \(itemsCrossed) <= \(itemsNotCrossed)")
  }
}

func isWithFarmer(item: String) -> Bool  {
  return itemPositions[item] ==  itemPositions["farmer"]
}

func move(item: String) {
  if itemPositions[item] == "crossed" {
    itemPositions["farmer"] = "not_crossed"
    itemPositions[item] = "not_crossed"
  } else {
    itemPositions["farmer"] = "crossed"
    itemPositions[item] = "crossed"
  }
  direction = (direction == "forward" ? "backward" : "forward")
}

func undoMove(item: String)  {
  if itemPositions[item] == "crossed" {
    itemPositions["farmer"] = "not_crossed"
    itemPositions[item] = "not_crossed"
  } else {
    itemPositions["farmer"] = "crossed"
```

```
      itemPositions[item] = "crossed"
    }
    direction = (direction == "forward" ? "backward" : "forward")
}

func isSafe() -> Bool {
  var itemsNotCrossed = [String]()
  var itemsCrossed = [String]()

  for (item, status) in itemPositions {
    if (status == "not_crossed") {
      itemsNotCrossed.append(item)
    } else {
      itemsCrossed.append(item)
    }
  }

  for _ in itemsNotCrossed {
    if !itemsNotCrossed.contains("farmer") {
      if itemsNotCrossed.contains("sheep") && itemsNotCrossed.contains("cabbage") {
          return false
      }
      if itemsNotCrossed.contains("sheep") && itemsNotCrossed.contains("wolf") {
          return false
      }
    }
  }

  for _ in itemsCrossed {
    if !itemsCrossed.contains("farmer") {
      if itemsCrossed.contains("sheep") && itemsCrossed.contains("cabbage") {
        return false
      }
      if itemsCrossed.contains("sheep") && itemsCrossed.contains("wolf") {
        return false
      }
    }
  }

  return true
}

func hasDoneBefore() -> Bool {
```

```
  for (_, entry) in movingLog {
    if (entry["farmer"] == itemPositions["farmer"] && entry["sheep"] == itemPositions["sh\
eep"] &&
        entry["wolf"] == itemPositions["wolf"] && entry["cabbage"] == itemPositions["cabb\
age"]) {
      return true
    }
  }
  return false
}

func cross() {

  if isAllCrossedRiver() {
    printMovingLog();
    print("Done")
    return // exit out of recursion
  }

  for item in items {
    if !isWithFarmer(item: item) {  // has to be move with farmer
      continue
    }

    if item == "farmer" && direction == "forward" { // no point just move farmer cross
      continue;
    }

    move(item: item);

    if isSafe() && !hasDoneBefore() {
      movingLog[step] = ["farmer": itemPositions["farmer"]!, "wolf": itemPositions["wolf"\
]!, "sheep": itemPositions["sheep"]!, "cabbage": itemPositions["cabbage"]! ];
      step += 1
      cross() // next step, recursive
    } else {
      undoMove(item: item)
    }
  }

}

cross();  // start the move
```

10.5 Cryptic Math Equation (Backtracking)

```swift
let letters = ["U", "K", "S", "A", "R", "G", "I", "N"]
var isDigitUsed = [0: false, 1: false, 2: false, 3: false, 4: false, 5: false, 6: false, \
7: false, 8: false, 9: false ]
var letterToDigits = [String: Int]() // Dictionary store the solution

func decodeLettersToNumber(letters: String, lookup: [String: Int]) -> Int {
  var str = letters
  for (k, v) in lookup {
      str = str.replacingOccurrences(of: k, with: String(v))
  }
  return Int(str)!;
}

func checkAnwer() {
  let uk = decodeLettersToNumber(letters: "UK", lookup: letterToDigits)
  let usa = decodeLettersToNumber(letters: "USA", lookup: letterToDigits)
  let ussr = decodeLettersToNumber(letters: "USSR", lookup: letterToDigits)
  let aging = decodeLettersToNumber(letters: "AGING", lookup: letterToDigits)
  if uk + usa + ussr  == aging {
    print("\(uk) + \(usa) + \(ussr) = \(aging)")
    print(letterToDigits)
  }
}

func solve(letterPosition: Int = 0) {

  if letterPosition == letters.count {  // got 8 letters filled
    checkAnwer()
    return
  }

  for i in 0...9 {    //# assign 0 - 9 to each letter
    if i == 0 && (letters[letterPosition] == "U" || letters[letterPosition] == "A") {
      continue
    }

    if letters[letterPosition] == "A" && i != 1 {
      continue
    }

    if letters[letterPosition] == "U" && i != 9 {
      continue
```

```
    }

    if letters[letterPosition] == "G" && i != 0 {
      continue
    }

    if isDigitUsed[i] == false {
      isDigitUsed[i] = true   // the number is used
      letterToDigits[letters[letterPosition]] = i
      solve(letterPosition: letterPosition + 1)   // move to next letter
      isDigitUsed[i] = false // clear
    }
  }
}

solve()
```

Chapter 11

```
@NSApplicationMain
class AppDelegate: NSObject, NSApplicationDelegate {

  @IBOutlet weak var window: NSWindow!

  @IBOutlet weak var text: NSTextField!

  func applicationDidFinishLaunching(_ aNotification: Notification) {
    // Insert code here to initialize your application
  }

  func applicationWillTerminate(_ aNotification: Notification) {
    // Insert code here to tear down your application
  }

  @IBAction func speak(_ sender: NSButton) {
    NSLog("Speak button clicked")

    let task: NSTask  = NSTask()
    task.launchPath = "/usr/bin/say"
    task.arguments = ["-v", "vicki", text.stringValue]
    task.launch()
```

```
    // the statement below will prevent do anything untils the tasks finishes
    task.waitUntilExit()
  }
}
```

Chapter 12

```
import UIKit

class ViewController: UIViewController {

  @IBOutlet weak var fromAmount: UITextField!
  @IBOutlet weak var euroAmount: UILabel!
  @IBOutlet weak var jpyAmount: UILabel!
  @IBOutlet weak var audAmount: UILabel!
  @IBOutlet weak var gbpAmount: UILabel!
  @IBOutlet weak var cnyAmount: UILabel!

  @IBOutlet weak var eurRateLabel: UILabel!
  @IBOutlet weak var eurReverseRateLabel: UILabel!
  @IBOutlet weak var jpyRateLabel: UILabel!
  @IBOutlet weak var jpyReverseRateLabel: UILabel!
  @IBOutlet weak var audRateLabel: UILabel!
  @IBOutlet weak var audReverseRateLabel: UILabel!
  @IBOutlet weak var gbpRateLabel: UILabel!
  @IBOutlet weak var gbpReverseRateLabel: UILabel!
  @IBOutlet weak var cnyRateLabel: UILabel!
  @IBOutlet weak var cnyReverseRateLabel: UILabel!

  var allCurrencies = ["AUD": "Australian Dollar", "USD": "US Dollar", "EUR": "Euro", "JP\
Y": "Japanese Yen", "CNY": "Chinese Yuan"]
  var cachedExchangeRateDict = [String: Double]()

  var currencyAmountUIDict =  [String: UILabel!]()
  var currencyRateUIDict =  [String: UILabel!]()
  var currencyReverseRateUIDict =  [String: UILabel!]()

  override func viewDidLoad() {
    super.viewDidLoad()
    // Do any additional setup after loading the view, typically from a nib.

    currencyAmountUIDict["EUR"] = euroAmount
```

```
    currencyAmountUIDict["AUD"] = audAmount
    currencyAmountUIDict["JPY"] = jpyAmount
    currencyAmountUIDict["GBP"] = gbpAmount
    currencyAmountUIDict["CNY"] = cnyAmount

    currencyRateUIDict["EUR"] = eurRateLabel
    currencyRateUIDict["JPY"] = jpyRateLabel
    currencyRateUIDict["AUD"] = audRateLabel
    currencyRateUIDict["GBP"] = gbpRateLabel
    currencyRateUIDict["CNY"] = cnyRateLabel

    currencyReverseRateUIDict["EUR"] = eurReverseRateLabel
    currencyReverseRateUIDict["JPY"] = jpyReverseRateLabel
    currencyReverseRateUIDict["AUD"] = audReverseRateLabel
    currencyReverseRateUIDict["GBP"] = gbpReverseRateLabel
    currencyReverseRateUIDict["CNY"] = cnyReverseRateLabel

    convert(sourceCurrency: "USD", sourceAmount: 100.0)
}

override func didReceiveMemoryWarning() {
  super.didReceiveMemoryWarning()
  // Dispose of any resources that can be recreated.
}

@IBAction func convertTapped(_ sender: AnyObject) {
  let amount = Double(fromAmount.text!)
  let currency = "USD" // hard code for now
  convert(sourceCurrency: currency, sourceAmount: amount!)
}

// converting
func convert(sourceCurrency: String, sourceAmount: Double) {

  for key in ["EUR", "AUD", "JPY", "GBP", "CNY"] {
    if (key == sourceCurrency) {
      continue
    }

    var rate : Double? = cachedExchangeRateDict["\(sourceCurrency)\(key)"]
    if (rate == nil) {
      // fetch from services
      rate = fetchExchangeRate(fromCurrency: sourceCurrency, toCurrency: key)
```

```
            cachedExchangeRateDict["\(sourceCurrency)\(key)"] = rate
        }

        let reverseRate = 1.0 / rate!

        let uiLabel   = currencyAmountUIDict[key]
        let uiRateLabel = currencyRateUIDict[key]
        let uiReverseRateLabel  = currencyReverseRateUIDict[key]

        let targetAmount = rate! * sourceAmount
        uiLabel!.text = formatAmount(number: (targetAmount as NSNumber))
        uiRateLabel!.text = "1 \(sourceCurrency) = \(rate!) \(key)"
        uiReverseRateLabel!.text = "1 \(key) = " + String(format:"%.4f", reverseRate) + " \\
(sourceCurrency)"
    }
  }

  func getURLContent(url: String) -> String {
    let urlContent : String = try! String(contentsOf: URL(string: url)!, encoding: String\
.Encoding.utf8)
    return urlContent
  }

  // deprecated, as Yahoo Finance API is down (or changed)
  func fetchExchangeRateYahooFinanceCSV(fromCurrency: String, toCurrency:String) -> Doubl\
e {
    let urlStr = "https://download.finance.yahoo.com/d/quotes.csv?" +
                "s=\(fromCurrency)\(toCurrency)=X&f=sl1d1t1ba&e=.csv"
    let rateCsvData = getURLContent(url: urlStr)
    let csvParagraphs = rateCsvData.components(separatedBy: ",")
    let exchangeRate = Double(csvParagraphs[1] as String)
    return exchangeRate!;
  }

  func fetchExchangeRateCurrentyConverterJSON(fromCurrency: String, toCurrency:String) ->\
 Double {
    let rateJSONData = getURLContent(url: "https://free.currencyconverterapi.com/api/v5/c\
onvert?q=" + fromCurrency + "_" + toCurrency + "&compact=y")
    let decoder = JSONDecoder()
    let decodedJson: [String: [String: Double]] = try! decoder.decode([String: [String: D\
ouble]].self, from: rateJSONData.data(using: .utf8)!)
    return decodedJson[fromCurrency + "_" + toCurrency]!["val"]!
  }
```

```swift
    func fetchExchangeRate(fromCurrency: String, toCurrency:String) -> Double {
        return fetchExchangeRateCurrentyConverterJSON(fromCurrency: fromCurrency, toCurrency:\
toCurrency);
    }

    func formatAmount(number:NSNumber) -> String{
        let formatter = NumberFormatter()
        formatter.numberStyle = .currency
        formatter.currencySymbol = ""                    // not currency symbol, e.g. $
        formatter.currencyGroupingSeparator = ","
        return formatter.string(from: number)!
    }

}
```

Resources

Solutions to exercises

http://zhimin.com/books/learn-swift-programming-by-examples[2]

Username: agileway
Password: CURRENCYWISE16

Log in with the above, or scan QR Code to acess directly.

Online resources

- **The Swift Programming Language Guide and Reference**[3]

  The official Swift language guide.
- **Raywenderlich Tutorials**[4]

  Good quality tutorials on Swift and App development.

Books

- **The Swift Programming Language**[5]

  The official Swift ebook from Apple.
- **Learn Ruby Programming by Examples**[6] by Zhimin Zhan and Courtney Zhan

  Learn Ruby programming to empower you to write scripts and cool web applications (Ruby on Rails). Master Ruby quickly by leveraging this book.
- **Cocoa Programming for OS X**[7] by Aaron Hillegass, Adam Preble and Nate Chandler, Big Nerd Ranch

  A good book on Cocoa programming.

---

[2]http://zhimin.com/books/learn-swift-programming-by-examples
[3]https://developer.apple.com/library/ios/documentation/Swift/Conceptual/Swift_Programming_Language/
[4]http://www.raywenderlich.com/tutorials
[5]https://itunes.apple.com/au/book/swift-programming-language/id881256329?mt=11
[6]https://leanpub.com/learn-ruby-programming-by-examples-en
[7]https://www.bignerdranch.com/we-write/cocoa-programming/

Software

- **CocoaPods**[8]

  CocoaPods is a long-standing dependency manager for Cocoa.
- **Carthage**[9]

  Alternative to CocoaPods, a simpler dependency manager.

---

[8]https://cocoapods.org/
[9]https://github.com/Carthage/Carthage